Contents

Like other words used by practitioners of espionage, tradecraft started as a euphemism for spycraft. Even though the term has roots in espionage, the principles and uses lend itself well outside that niche. Tradecraft is a broad term, which encompasses all techniques, methods, skills, and technologies to conceal and protect sensitive activities or relationships from an opponent. Developing tradecraft can be daunting, because governments and criminal organizations spent the last century continuously improving their methods to detect it. This book seeks to set up a foundation of information to conduct clandestine activities in areas controlled by an oppressive adversary.

The intended audience of this book are those who are called to work in oppressive regions of the world; particularly, journalists, missionaries, and liberators, who find themselves in an asymmetric fight. The United States' Declaration of Independence says the Creator endowed <u>all</u> people with certain unalienable rights. If the author believes that to be true, then these freedoms cannot end at the borders of the United States. Citizens of the world have the rights of religion, association, speech, and press, and should not endure the suppression thereof in whatever form it may take.

Granted, many of these oppressed peoples will not have access to this resource, let alone many other resources; however, the author trusts the benevolent citizens of the United States will continue to go forth and risk their physical selves to spread the the same liberties abroad. Going forward, this book offers tools to help them succeed and stay safe.

This book attempts to help those who wish to contribute to the world in a greater sense than themselves. Too often these altruistic people are horribly under-prepared when facing dangerous adversaries. They are decapitated or mutilated by extremists and oppressors as loved ones watch helplessly at home, because they lacked the proper skills, planning, and preparation needed to succeed in their endeavors.

Then there is the concern of whether the nefarious can use this knowledge. The answer is: Yes. While it is true this information may make it difficult for authorities to stop bad actors, the sad truth is these people already have their own tradecraft. In fact, tradecraft is ubiquitous around the world and among society's institutions. It is only the average person who is not privy to these techniques. Intelligence agencies, special operations forces, criminal enterprises, militant extremists, politicians, and hackers all have methods to keep their relationships and activities secret. This book presents nothing new to them.

The content inside does not derive from any one nation or organization's methods, but a culmination of many. It pulls from governmental, criminal, and militant techniques without regard to nationality. This book originated from the study of many works, ranging from declassified U.S. Office of Strategic Services and British Special Operations Executive field manuals and intelligence reports, to more recent articles and various military field manuals. This book sought to analyze, extrapolate, synthesize, and distill that information into digestible modules. The reader can choose the methods he needs to carry out his goals by studying the relevant chapters.

The book describes adversaries throughout, but isn't alluding to any specific organizations. With advancements in technology and sharing of knowledge, many of the capabilities described within are no longer unique to sophisticated or well-funded government agencies. Now, the poorest of governments and criminal organization can own these capabilities.

Over the decades, hackers, criminals, and operatives passed their tradecraft and lessons learned to each other to a point where this information is available with a web browser and internet connection, or through consumer publications. The last thing for any clandestine actor to understand is his adversary's specific capabilities, and then tailor his tradecraft to it.

This book uses the masculine pronoun simply for brevity and is not implying that only males could, should, or would be the only gender that executes these activities. To the contrary, from what the author has seen and learned, it is indistinguishable between the sexes as to who conducts these activities more. Even in the Bible, the safehouse keeper who helped the Israelite spies in Jericho was a woman. Do not let the use of the masculine pronoun distract from the knowledge contained within this book.

This is the second edition of this book. It was revised for spelling, grammar, and flow. The primary content remains unchanged other than the removal of the external references and descriptions of courses. For those who are looking to contact author, please email **RaspProject@protonmail.com**.

Most operations have a similar life cycle. These phases include: planning, preparation, and execution. Due to the inherent risk of clandestine operations, a planner must include contingencies for when things do not go according to plan. In this context, contingencies are bad. This chapter introduces some recurrent concepts, and then discusses the phases of the operational cycle and contingencies.

The book uses the term "Principal" throughout to describe the person who is accountable for the success of the operation. The Principal is often a foreigner to the target area, and recruits others, referred to as "Residents", to carry out the operational goals. A Resident is often a local or someone who is already an established part of the target area.

One cannot stress the importance of planning enough. It is no small task, and requires much foresight and work. The first step of planning is defining the goals of the operation, which must have a fixed and focused end. If the Principal does not explicitly name his goals, then he may find himself in a position he cannot escape or may not finish what he started.

Before the Principal starts dedicating resources and time to an operation, he must first perform a risk-versus-gain assessment. This helps keep the operation focused, especially when the Principal comes across obstacles, be it financial, legal, adversarial, ethical, or similar. The Principal answers what would happen if the operation was successful, and what he would stand to lose if the attempt failed. The Principal then decides whether he possesses the time, effort, and resources required to succeed in this endeavor, and if expense would still be worth the try even in failure. To help make this decision, the Principal gathers as much intelligence as he can.

Intelligence collection is a broad topic. Each intelligence discipline can, and often does, call for its own book or series. This will be a topical overview of what could apply to the Principal. The Principal will collect information from public sources, human sources, and the Principal's own observations. Each of these sources will feed into each other to form a fuller, multi-dimensional understanding of the Principal's subject, so he can become a subject matter expert.

Intelligence collection is something a Principal must do always. He collects intelligence before starting an operation to decide whether to pursue it, and continues collecting throughout the duration of the operation. The book discusses the reasons and collection methods throughout.

Public source, or open source, is information derived from publicly available sources, as the name states. In the intelligence world, this is known as Open Source Intelligence, or OSINT for short. OSINT for the Principal includes publications like internet and newspaper articles, books, imagery, and so on. OSINT is much more robust than what this chapter describes, due to the internet and advanced systems that comb and analyze data. However, the Principal is not likely to have such capabilities. Chapter two further discusses OSINT as a threat.

The Principal often starts with a search engine, and reads and studies as many publications as possible about his subject. As the Principal learns, he begins to find intelligence gaps. His queries become more refined, and he starts recognizing reliable sources of knowledge. One of the greatest benefits of the internet age is the breadth and depth of knowledge available. Because many have already done much in the world and throughout history, content creators are encouraged to get very specific with their published works in order to distinguish themselves from others. The Principal now has access to almost any knowledge base imaginable.

The more the Principal researches, the more he finds what information applies to his subject. Even if an article or book does not directly answer a question, the Principal gets more context as he reads. This information comes together in new and beneficial ways. This will also help him find potential human sources, and tailor his questions to them.

There will be questions that publications cannot answer. Open sources are static media, and the Principal will eventually want sources that can answer his questions directly. This leads to human sources, which is known in the intelligence community as Human Intelligence, or HUMINT for short.

There are four ways humans gather information: observation, acquisition, participation, and solicitation. The definitions below use the contents of a book to illustrate the how human sources obtain knowledge.

Observation obtains information about the subject material directly through the source's senses. If the Principal asks the Resident how he knows the contents of a book, the Resident says he read it. Remember: This relies on the interpretation and memory of the Resident.

Acquisition obtains either the original or a copy of the subject material. If the Principal asks the Resident for the details of a book, the Resident would deliver a copy of it. As reliable as this is, it is the riskiest due to the possession of compromising materials.

Participation obtains information due to a direct role in the creation of the subject details. If the Principal asks the Resident how he knows the details of the book, the Resident would say he wrote it. This is also risky due to the nature of having a relationship with someone involved with sensitive activities.

Solicitation obtains information from another person. This sub-source could have seen the information or took part in its creation, and then tells the Resident. If the Principal asks the

Resident how he knows the details of the book, the Resident would say he heard it from someone else. This relies on two or more individuals' memory and interpretation before it is reaches the Principal. This is the least reliable, but the most common way people collect information.

When researching, the Principal should note the authors of the publications, and seek to understand the context in which the authors learned of the subject matter and the authors' motivations for writing. When the Principal exhausts these publications of their value, he tries to contact these authors to fill any gaps he may have.

The Principal should always get the source's source of information. If the source knows the material because of his personal experience, then that testimony carries weight. If the source obtained it from a sub-source, then the Principal should attempt to exploit the sub-source himself, because the source might not have interpreted the information correctly.

The Principal does not limit his human sources to authors. Each Resident is a source of information, even if his job is not information gathering. Every time the Principal meets a Resident, the Principal should ask about the climate surrounding the operation. Not understanding these different perspectives is guarantying failure.

Lastly, the Principal will use his personal observations as a means of collecting intelligence. Whether he starts a mission to explicitly collect information or just goes about his cover life, he must stay vigilant and situationally aware.

The next step in planning is assessing resources. Operations are expensive. They need time, money, support, equipment, and sacrifice. The Principal knows all he must give, and whether that would be enough to satisfy his goals. If he cannot meet the operational needs, he must decide if he can get it. The Principal may use his cover occupation to fund clandestine activities; otherwise, he may need sponsors who can fill these resource gaps.

The Principal must assess his personal skills. He may not have all the skills needed to complete this type of operation initially. The Principal must work on his weaknesses. If the Principal is challenged to keep track of vehicles and people during counter-surveillance, then he conducts mental exercises to help him develop those memory skills.

A part of knowing the Principal's goals is knowing where he will pursue them. The Principal must assess the target area and how certain factors affect his operation. These assessment factors include social, historical, political, economic, legal, and regulatory.

Social factors include the language spoken, religion, social graces, etiquette, and proper relationships between the various demographics, religions, genders, and classes. This is important for how, when, and where the Principal will develop relationships with locals in both a cover and operational context. Not abiding by these restrictions may jeopardize the operation, or turn people against the Principal.

Understanding where the society is coming from will go a long way in understanding why the people of a society behave and believe the way they do. Furthermore, understanding the historical context of an area and discussing it intelligently will aid in rapport building. Rapport is crucial in garnering support for the Principal's goals.

The Principal must understand the political challenges the society faces. Politics tie into both the social and historical contexts of how the society seeks to make themselves more prosperous. If the Principal's goals aid in the accomplishment of some political or ideological end, then he may find support from others.

The economy is important in that it affects the priorities of a society and decides how far the Principal's resources will go.

First, the more impoverished an area, the less they will care or support more ideological goals. Few poor or oppressed nations care about the social acceptance of non-binary genders. They care more about when they will eat next and from where that food may come. This helps the Principal understand where his goals lie in terms of the local priorities.

Next, the Principal's financial resources can have a greater impact in impoverished regions than more affluent ones. However, the more economically downtrodden the area, the more crime exists. The more desperate people get, the less moral they become. This can have a significant impact on the threats the Principal may face.

Nations differ with the laws they have and the regulations that guide how their laws are executed. Where one nation may find something acceptable, another may find gravely not. This is important for the activities, equipment, and relationships the Principal expects to do or have. Other chapters will discuss this concept and how it pertains to their respective topics.

These factors lead to the environmental permissiveness of the area. Permissiveness relates to how scrutinized the Principal may be in a region, community, or society. This may not be an issue for Residents as they are already an established part of the society, unless the Resident is prominent. There are three levels of permissiveness: permissive, semi-permissive, and non-permissive.

Permissive environments are those where **neither** the locals nor authorities oppose the Principal's presence or activities.

Semi-permissive environments are those where **either** the locals or the authorities oppose the Principal's presence or activities.

Non-permissive environments are those where **both** the locals and the authorities oppose the Principal's presence or activities.

The Principal should seek permissive environments to contact Residents when he can, and must not work in non-permissive environments.

Permissiveness for a Resident is similar for the Principal, but locals and authorities do not necessarily oppose the Resident's presence or activities; rather, depending how prominent or social the Resident is, the locals or authorities may know, track, and share this information among themselves. Less permissive environments for a Resident may draw scrutiny from the community to any relationships the Resident has, including one with the Principal.

The book uses the term "Adversary" to describe any person or group that could and would negatively affect the outcome of the Principal's operation. Three factors characterize an Adversary: authority, intelligence, and jurisdiction.

Authority is the ability to render the Principal incapable of continuing his clandestine activities, like homicide, detention, or seizure. Intelligence is the ability to find, know, and track individuals and groups. Jurisdiction is the geographic reach in terms of authority and intelligence.

The Principal must gather information about his Adversary's strengths, weaknesses, and methods of operation. This includes personnel strength, frequented locations and routes, schedules, morale, relationships with locals and authorities, equipment, maintenance, tactics, goals, plans, hierarchy, and so on. The Principal seeks to know which of the above elements help or hinder the Adversary's ability to carry out its goals.

The Principal must know how the Adversary would: a) react to discovering the Principal, b) gather this information, c) conduct an investigation, and d) ultimately incapacitates the Principal. Eventually, the Principal comes up with enemy courses of action, which helps him design his tradecraft to mitigate these threats.

If the Adversary is violent, the Principal must find areas deemed sanctuary. This can be an area or region where the Adversary does not have jurisdiction, either through opposition or limited resources. In impoverished or oppressive regions, it may be a neighboring country. The Principal must research the environments, climates, and adversarial activities and tactics he may come across getting from the target area to sanctuary. The ratline chapter discusses this in more detail.

If the Principal feels there is an injustice in the world, there may be others who feel the same way. In the least, the Principal may find that the enemies of his enemy are his friends. The Principal gathers information about these potential friendlies like he did for the Adversary. In addition, the Principal understands friendly motivations and whether they are something to which he can contribute.

After the Principal conducts his preliminary intelligence campaign and decides to move forward with his operation, he begins looking for potential Residents. Much of this the Principal can only do in person, but for more prominent or support Residents, the Principal may start dossiers on those he can research from afar. This is especially true for business owners and others who work in the target area as foreigners. Examples are bush pilots in Africa or mariners in East Asia who run supplies for missions or profit. They own a valuable resource of transportation that the Principal may find critical.

The Principal must decide which forms of communication will help coordinate and carry out his goals for both support and operational Residents. This will aid in the decision of what skills and equipment he will need to be successful. Other chapters will go much deeper into this topic.

Once the Principal has a good understanding of the above factors, he begins deciding on the more day-to-day details. The Principal should select a residence that will offer a buffer between his cover activities and his operational ones. The Principal avoids areas where he may meet operational Residents. This will avoid chance encounters, which could jeopardize other parts of the operation.

Transportation is a key consideration for any operation. Some areas may afford private transportation, others may not, especially if it makes the Principal stand out. Regulations and the Principal's resources also play a role in what transportation the Principal can use. This will also affect the type of contact the Principal will make with Residents. If he cannot obtain a vehicle, then he may not host vehicular meetings.

The Principal decides on what equipment he needs to carry out his goals. This can include cameras, phones, computers, GPS, USB drives, compasses, maps, and so on. If it is readily accessible, then he may buy it in-country. If such equipment is unavailable, rare, or illegal, then he may not use it. If it is critical, then he finds a way to bring it in, and stores it safely.

It is important to note that some technologies are not legal in every country. Russia, China, and India have restrictions on the use of encryption. Possession of such technology is punishable. The same goes for weapons; most nations outlaw firearms.

When the Principal considers the above, he must start mapping and planning what he will do, and when, where, and how he will do it. The Principal decides on the schedules and routes he will take throughout the operation. The above factors and decisions will play a role in how he travels from his cover residence to the operational area, and when he will dedicate time to a cover and to clandestine activities. This helps him get an idea for his cover and avoid potential threats.

Then the Principal beings to design his cover. This considers all the above factors and decisions, and enables him to safely and securely carry out his goals. The covers chapter will discuss this more.

The last step of planning is creating a road map from beginning to end. The Principal will outline, as specifically as he can, his tour from start to finish. One way of doing this is backwards planning, which is to start with what he wants to do, and work his way back through the prerequisites to where he is now. Then he would run through the plan forward to ensure that his plan works out logically and logistically. This chapter discusses the elements of this road map in the following sections.

The next phase is preparation. The Principal will do some steps before deployment, some step after entering the area, and other steps throughout the operation. It will depend on whether the preparatory step is a prerequisite to doing a task, and whether the Principal can complete it at that time. The Principal does not procrastinate, rather, prepares for his tasks as early as possible. This will make him more flexible in the event obstacles or changes arise.

The following are some steps the Principal may take before deploying:

Many who read this book may not have all skills needed to successfully complete a clandestine operation. After the Principal understands what skills he needs, he seeks to master them. This is often done through research and practice. Some skills may need supervision, so the Principal seeks courses to hone his skills.

Crafting, backstopping, and seasoning covers is a lengthy process. Some of which the Principal can do before entering the target area. If a cover needs another profession, education, training, or certification, then the Principal should do so early on, as that may take more time, effort, and money than most preparatory steps. The covers chapter discusses this topic much more.

If the Principal wants sponsors to fund his activities, then he must find and set up relationships with those sponsors. This is akin to getting investors for a business venture. Doing so is outside the scope of this book.

Depending on what equipment is available and how the Principal can get it, the Principal may get what he needs before deploying. Most of the Principal's equipment should support his cover, as the first weeks in country are when the Adversary and locals scrutinize the Principal the most. After circumstances return to normal, the Principal may get the rest of the equipment he needs to complete his goals.

A key part of preparation is getting visas for the regions in which he works and to where he would escape. This is something he cannot neglect and ensures are current. The ratline chapter further discusses this.

At this point, the Principal knows where he should lay his head at night and how he will get around. The Principal decides whether to makes reservations before entering the area or use shopping as a reason for counter-surveillance. Either way, not choosing the best locations or vehicles gives the Principal a reason for change if the operation or security calls for it.

The next section discusses those preparatory steps the Principal does after deploying to the target area.

The next phase of an operation is execution. In this phase, the Principal deploys to the target area, sets up the support infrastructure and relationships, completes his goals, and returns home alive.

The Principal made his way to the target area. He packed his bags, boarded the plane or boat, and set foot inside the target area. The Principal is now in a state of uncertainty.

For the first few weeks in the target area, the Principal assumes everyone scrutinizes him and all that he does. Therefore, the Principal must not perform any compromising activities during this period.   This period ends when the Principal confidently decides others no longer scrutinize him.

During this time, the Principal limits himself to only those activities that are not compromising, which include casing, spotting for Residents, backstopping and seasoning his cover, and establishing natural patterns.

Casing is deciding whether a location is suitable for operational use.   Casing results in the Principal's abilities to predict whether that location is conducive to conduct some operational activity. At this point the Principal knows what types of locations he needs for operational functions. The Principal gathers enough data and information about these locations to confidently predict whether that location is suitable at the proposed time of using it.   There are two phases to casing: map reconnaissance and personal reconnaissance.

Map reconnaissance is researching areas of interest via records and documents to add or remove potentially suitable locations. This is not only using maps, as the term implies, but includes other open sources to understand more about those locations and the areas that surround them.   However, map reconnaissance is never enough.

Personal reconnaissance is uncompromisingly necessary. Many believe that a good "Google Recon" is enough, when in fact it is far from it. Personal reconnaissance is necessary for two reasons: even the more current documents and records may not be current enough, such is the case for web-based mapping applications, and the authors of those records and documents did not create them by casing for clandestine activities. A couple of examples include how buildings change businesses, like from a store to a bank, or how proprietors of these locations add certain security measures, like cameras or guards.

The Principal assesses operational locations by applying the exposure and logic principles. Exposure is physical in nature, while logic is psychological in nature.

Exposure relates to how a subject must stimulate the observer's senses to acknowledge the subject's existence. There are two ways to affect exposure: physical obstruction and duration of observability. In terms of security, duration depends on obstruction: the more obstruction, the more time available for contact.

Logic is whether the subject will stay in the observer's memory once he sees and acknowledges the subject. An observer often disregards or forgets an ordinary subject quickly. However, an observer remembers and may discuss rare, bizarre, or troubling occurrence. Just as duration is to obstruction, so is logic to exposure. The more exposure to an observer, the more the contact needs logic in appearance and behavior.

While casing may start in this phase, the Principal will case throughout the duration the operation. Each chapter discusses its own casing considerations.

Spotting is searching for people who could successfully perform some task or function necessary for the operation. After the Principal decides with what he needs help, spotting is the step that builds a list of such candidates. The next step is assessment, which this section discusses later.

Making a list of potential Residents derives from the intelligence gathered about a target or understanding the context of an operational goal. The more the Principal discovers about a target through OSINT, direct observations, and eventually HUMINT, the more he will notice people who can help him succeed in his goals. For example, if a journalist discovers his target frequents a certain restaurant to discuss sensitive topics, then the Principal would spot for staff who may overhear conversations of interest.

Seasoning a cover is using it by living and wearing it. Depending on the circumstances, the Principal may need to do some backstopping, which is creating and putting into place evidence that supports his cover. The Principal tries to do as much of the backstopping as he can before deployment, but there may be some elements to the cover that he can only backstop after. He seasons and backstops while he is deciding whether he is still under scrutiny.

Lastly, the Principal sets up his natural patterns, which are the locations, schedules, and activities he wishes others will come to expect from him. The Principal incorporates casing, spotting, and cover seasoning to help build his natural patterns, so those areas, times, and behaviors do not raise suspicions later. The covers chapter discusses this more.

Once the Principal decides his natural patterns are well established, where people no longer take interest in his presence or activities, he starts setting up his support infrastructure. The support infrastructure includes those relationships, sites, caches, and ratlines that will ensure the Principal can complete his operation and make it home alive. These activities are not completely clandestine, but if discovered would lead the Adversary to investigate the Principal. These activities include: approaching and assessing support Residents, caching, equipment acquisition, and setting up ratlines.

At this point, the Principal only approaches and assesses support Residents. Prematurely approaching an operational Resident before the Principal establishes the support infrastructure, may put the Principal in a situation he cannot escape.

The Principal must separate Residents in support roles from operational roles. Support Residents should not be in anyway involved with nor have a reason to hide from the Adversary. The Principal must not try to reuse operational Residents for support tasks. Support roles are separate from operational roles, and must stay that way for security, also known as compartmentalization.

The beginning of any relationship with a Resident is the initial pretext, which is the circumstances of how the Principal and Resident first meet. There is much that goes into this setup, first being a preliminary investigation.

Once the Principal has a list of Residents, he starts an investigation for each one to decide which Residents offer the greatest chance of success to complete the proposed task or function. These investigations follow a principle known as least-to-most intrusive. It starts with methods which offer the least interference and risk, and progresses to methods which are more sensitive or aggressive.

First, the Principal will try to gather information about a Resident through OSINT, like licenses, social media, and so on. Then the Principal may include surveillance, eliciting from associates, and dumpster-diving to get a better understanding of who the target is. The last phase is often approaching the target directly, such as elicitation. As the Principal gathers more information about a Resident, he assesses them and decides whether they would be good candidates for recruitment. If the Principal discovers something about the Resident that makes him unsuitable, the Principal stops the investigation and moves on to another candidate.

If the Principal decides a Resident is worth approaching, he must select a proper pretext to approach him. The goal of this initial pretext is to put the Principal and Resident into a situation where a relationship will blossom. This may not be a one-time effort, as the Principal may choose to increment his presence into the Resident's life over time. Depending on the type of operation, the Resident may soon discover that the Principal thinks, acts, and believes the same as the Resident does: The Resident discovers a new best friend.

When the Principal assess a Resident, he keeps three questions in mind: would, could, and should the Resident do what the Principal asks?

Would: This is by far the most crucial factor in clandestine operations. Often, it is a matter of finding people who are willing to do something as a Principal can often teach or fabricate the other factors of capability and suitability. Approaching the wrong person can often expose the Principal to hostilities well beyond any other factor, so it is important that he pays attention to a potential Resident's motivations before and after recruitment. The Principal may find many who could, but only a few actually would.

There are several approaches to understanding the psychological motivations of someone who is willing to face adversity for someone else. There are: The Money, Ideology, Compassion, and Ego (MICE) model, the Maslow's Hierarchy of Needs model, and the Reciprocation, Authority, Scarcity, Commitment, Consistency, Liking, Social-Proof (RASCCLS) model.

Regardless of the model, there are three component-needs, which alleviate internal conflict. They are: psychological, material, and emotional. If one or more of these needs conflict with others, then it becomes difficult to predict the Resident's behavior.

Psychological needs often grant purpose. The Resident must be psychologically in tune with what the Principal is trying to do. While the Principal can buy allegiances, that is often superficial and unreliable. The moment the Resident faces adversity, he leaves. There is little point of earning money if one cannot spend it. The Principal wants someone who believes with their logical faculty that what he is doing is just and right.

Material needs are how people live. This is often manifested as money, as that is how people obtain food, shelter, clothes, luxuries, and vices. If what the Principal asks of the Resident becomes a burden on the Resident financially or materialistically, to the point of sacrifice, it will become an unbearable stress. There is a balance when it comes to supplying material needs. Too much, and people tend to get greedy or lazy, too little and people feel taken advantage of. The Principal seeks to meet the Resident's perceived needs, and then some extra to allow for a bit of luxury, but nothing too extravagant from his current personal circumstance. This will also lead to setting up an emotional bond.

Emotional needs are something that people must feel to own loyalty. Even if the Resident believes in the same ideologies and has his material needs met, unless the Resident has a personal, heartfelt tie, then adversity will shatter the relationship. Emotional needs, or compassion, is often the result of reciprocity, liking, commitment, or similar. Helping another in a time of need or lifting a burden makes comrades. If the Principal can be that personal savior, then he will have a reliable, loyal friend –at least until the Principal becomes a burden and the Resident repays the debt.

Could: This is purely about the ability to successfully do what the Principal asks. The Resident must own the necessary knowledge, skills, abilities, and equipment to succeed. Not only basic skills, but further skills to overcome expected obstacles in the real mission.

When it comes to whether someone could perform the required task, the Resident must own the intestinal fortitude to execute what the Principal needs him to under the mission's specific circumstances. Some people are willing and seem to be a perfect candidate; however, when the going gets tough, some people just cannot perform. The Principal must devise a test to figure out how the Resident would handle the stresses he would face during the mission.

Should: Has two considerations: reliability and morals. While could decides whether mission success is possible, should decides whether it is probable.

Reliability is the determining factor for probability, and has many considerations including: personal circumstances, plans and goals, and discipline.

Personal circumstances involve obligations to one's family, work, and society. The Principal should assess the priority of these circumstances in comparison to what the Principal needs the Resident to do, and when the Resident must do it. If under no circumstance will the Resident sacrifice his weekends with his children, then the task or function should either avoid that sacred time or the Principal finds someone who is more suitable.

Plans and Goals: many often overlook them. The Principal needs to know if the Resident will be around when needed. The Principal ensures the Resident is not moving or selling needed equipment before a task or function is performed. The Principal desires reliability, and if he must recruit a replacement, then he should do so in a way that minimizes the lack of coverage as much as possible.

Discipline is paramount. The Resident must perform to a standard regardless of how he feels at the time. This is important in facing adversity, but also in how the Resident approaches life. Many people who are incredibly gifted still lack discipline and drive to get them where they need to be. If the Resident is perpetually late, lax in his assessments or performance, then he has discipline issues.

Morals: The other half of "should" discusses the morals of recruiting the Resident. This ranges from the Resident's demographics to the repercussions of what may happen if the Adversary catches the Resident. The Principal must answer whether he could live with himself knowing that the Resident understood full well and accepted the risks. The Principal must not do anything he will later regret, like recruit a child or ask someone to unwittingly accept the risks of torture or homicide.

The last step in acquiring a Resident is recruitment. This is outside the scope of this book. There are many other publications that cover this, even in the context of clandestine relationships.

The last steps of setting up support infrastructure are caching and setting up ratlines. The respective chapters discuss these in much detail.

After the Principal establishes support infrastructure, he moves on to operational goals. Even though it seems like there was much work performed up to this point, the Principal is less than or equal to 50% done with his operation, depending on his goals. This next part of the operation includes: assessing, approaching, and recruiting operational Residents, and completing the Develop-Task-Train-Deploy-Recover-Exploit cycle several times until the Principal meets his goals, or exhausts his resources.

To make a long explanation shorter, the Principal must apply the same level of assessment, development, and training he did for himself to the Resident. The Principal is responsible for the success of the operation, which means he is also responsible for the success of each Resident.

Once the operation accomplishes its goals, the Principal must conclude his activities. This includes ending the relationships, dissolving or liquidating the assets, and making his way out of the target area.

Depending on operational goals, the Principal may setup redundant Resident operations to ensure success. If one or a few Resident operations accomplish the goals before the others, the Principal needs to shut the others down, even if incomplete.

Terminating a relationship is outside the scope of this book. However, it is important to note that the Principal satisfies his promises to his Residents, and reiterates the importance of secrecy and finality of the relationship.

After the Principal concludes his relationships, he must close his cover life in a smooth and natural manner. The Principal can either build in a limit to the cover, like an expiring visa or contract, or he can have another catalyst that gives him a graceful exit. For those covers that acquired assets throughout the operation, like a business, vehicle, residence, and so on, the Principal liquidates those assets or agreements. Doing this may keep the Adversary from becoming suspicious. Even if the

Principal leaves the target area, it does not mean all his associates are safe.

After the closure, the Principal boards a plane or boat and goes home.

The previous section described how an operation would flow if everything followed the plan; however, humans make mistakes. If there were no threats from an Adversary, then this book would be unnecessary. Whether the Principal, a Resident, or bad luck leads to compromise, the Principal needs to plan for it.

Adversarial awareness is a concept that relates to the risk of discovery. There are three awareness phases through which the Adversary may transition during an operation: ignorance, probing, and targeting.

Ignorance is the complete unawareness of clandestine activities. This is where the Principal works successfully: he cases, caches, meets, and facilitates his operation. Tradecraft tries to keep the Adversary in this phase with the use of natural patterns, covers, and communication techniques.

Probing is a preliminary investigation to decide whether a claim of clandestine activities has merit. If a claim does have merit, the Adversary moves on to the targeting phase; otherwise, they move back to the ignorance phase. Tradecraft seeks to detect this phase-shift, and protects the operation from more intrusive scrutiny. The Principal does this through counter-surveillance, caching, and covers. If the Principal detects any form of surveillance, he aborts any further clandestine action, resorts to his cover, and eventually makes his way out of the Adversary's jurisdiction.

Targeting is after probing, and the Adversary decides the claim of clandestine activities has merit. The Adversary is now seeking enough evidence to persecute the Principal and all his associated Residents. If the Adversary reaches this phase, the

Principal neither detected nor protected against the probing phase; any continued presence in the area is extremely dangerous. Tradecraft tries to circumvent this hostile situation with a ratline.

While least-to-most intrusive is a general investigative principle, the Adversary may not follow it. Adversaries may conduct a couple of interviews, burglarize a residence or work, or jump straight to interrogation. The Adversary's resources, morals, or professionalism decide their process of investigation. Many Western governments have an abundance of resources, their citizenry holds their agencies accountable, and are very competent and professional. These governments may progress through many phases of investigation and spend gratuitous amounts of money to collect the necessary evidence. Contrast this with militant extremists or criminal organizations who murder suspects based on emotion, pomp, biased testimony, or uncorroborated or circumstantial evidence.

The Principal is wise to set up an early warning system, which notifies the Principal of any imminence of hostility. Sources of this information include: all recruited Residents, direct observations, and OSINT. OSINT sources include radio, television, newspapers, and embassy alerts. The goal is getting information about impending threats before hostiles put the Principal in any situation he cannot escape.

Chapter 2: Covers

Covers are by far the most important and impactful aspect of tradecraft. Having an ostensible reason for traveling, meeting people, building relationships, and passing information can protect the Principal and his operation much more than limiting the possibility of people witnessing any clandestine activities. Therefore, the Principal should always strive to create or keep strong, reliable covers throughout everything he does.

First, some common terms and concepts:

Natural covers rely on the truth of a wearer's circumstances to conceal his relationships and activities. These covers rely on omission instead of lies to protect clandestine activities.

Artificial covers are fabricated facts and records about the wearer. The wearer might not fabricate his entire cover, but at least one detail is. The cover depends on one or more lies and false evidence for security.

Assumed covers are when a subject has proper natural cover or circumstances to further an operation, but for whatever reason he cannot, or will not take part. The wearer then dawns this identity to carry out a mission.

Status covers are the reasons the Principal is present in a target area. These answer all questions that derive from someone scrutinizing the Principal, whether hostile or innocent. This scrutiny may include basic interrogatives of the Principal's historical context, current circumstances, and future goals.

Action covers are reasons for the wearer's behavior derived from clandestine actions. The action covers will need to answer the basic interrogatives and follow up questions associated with these behaviors.

Relationship covers are the ostensible reasons for an association between the Principal and one or more of his

Residents. The cover should pay attention to the start of the relationship and the reasons why the relationship continues. All too often these covers neglect logic and testing.

Second-tier covers are the reasons why the wearer lied after the initial cover failed. When selecting second-tier covers, it is important the Principal chooses a reason for lying that carries a more lenient punishment than the clandestine activity. This can be optional, especially if the consequence of the clandestine activity is marking the Principal persona non-grata.

Props are documents, effects, articles, or items that help support the cover if scrutinized. The wearer possesses props that a reasonable person would expect for an activity, or those that can strengthen a cover. These include business cards, receipts from ostensibly visited establishments, notes, and so on. The Principal uses props to aid relationship covers. If the Principal is an investor and the Resident is an entrepreneur, then they should have the proper documents.

Backstopping is the process that ensures the wearer's claims satisfy any verification activities an adversary may conduct. This includes proof of legal documents (licenses, visas, sponsorships), infrastructure (websites, phone numbers, offices), relationships (employees, students, customers), testimony and so on.

Seasoning is living the cover, and is a part of backstopping. As the community views the Principal and his activities, and the cover becomes common knowledge. If the Adversary canvases the area for an investigation, it gathers consistent testimony in support of the Principal's cover.

Sanitization is the process of removing compromising articles from the wearer's possession for which he has no logical explanation. This mean the Principal either caches these items or puts them in a concealment device. If the Adversary scrutinizes the wearer, then these items do not compromise the operation.

Covers convince an inquirer that the clandestine activities are normal and non-threatening. A cover counters three approaches an adversary may use to discover these activities: direct questioning of the Principal and his Residents, asking third parties, or Open Source Intelligence (OSINT).

Direct Questioning, as the name suggests, is when the Adversary, or an agent thereof, explicitly asks the Principal or his Residents about who he is, what he is doing, and why he is doing it. There is no real trickery, despite attempts to elicit contradictions in a story by backing the interviewee into a corner. Therefore, it is important to have a well-planned and rehearsed cover. The Principal must poke holes in the cover stories to expose any illogical elements, and then address them.

When executed well, direct questioning can be quite daunting for the interviewee. An interviewer only needs the basic interrogatives to be successful. When used properly and relentlessly, these simple questions can extract awesome amounts of detail. The key to a successful cover story, is to know what is realistic and proper in terms of depth and breadth of knowledge. There is a fine balance between not knowing enough and knowing too much. The Principal and his Residents must practice defending their covers and pay attention to the proper level of detail.

Covers should not sound so rehearsed that it is obviously so. A nice balance is going through the motions of what the cover suggests. This way, it is not fabricated thoughts, but memory recollection. For example, if the Principal is working on a cover business, he should go through all the steps of starting a business: writing and pitching proposals, raising capital, searching for vendors, marketing, and so on. This way, the Principal can talk intelligently, make connections, backstop, and season the cover all at once.

This method also helps strengthen relationship covers, a sometimes-weak link in clandestine activities. By having both the Principal and Resident perform the activities claimed, it is much easier and more secure to defend the cover. By both describing what they saw and did, they avoid sounding rehearsed. The security comes from omitting clandestine details and offering as much of the cover details as asked.

It also helps if the Principal and Resident set aside time during each contact to discuss and role-play cover elements, such as arguing, collaborating, or negotiating details of an agreement. This helps relationship maintain a natural evolution after each meeting.

The Principal should not neglect cover progress of the relationship. If the Principal claims he is helping someone, then he must help them in a way that offers evidence and progression. If the relationship's purpose is starting a business, then there should be reasonable benchmarks and schedules to which the cover relationship should adhere.

Soliciting from third parties can either come from people approaching the Adversary or the other way around, for example: informing or eliciting, respectively. Many investigators have sources positioned throughout the community and are knowledgeable of gossip or newsworthy events. A competent Adversary further investigates any changes to the status quo, such as the Principal entering the area, developing relationships with locals, or if a Resident has illogically changed his behaviors or patterns.

To counter these approaches, the Principal uses covers to satisfy curiosities without raising questions. The Principal should neither broadcast his covers nor avoid their deployment. There is no way to erase all evidence of clandestine activities. The Principal holds meetings, loads and unloads dead drops, and emplaces and retrieves caches. Friends, family, and associates will miss both the Principal's and Resident's presence. A cover just gives a reason for those outward-facing behaviors. When asked, the Principal and Residents should not hide or shy away; rather, they should reveal as much detail as if the covers were truth, no more and no less.

OSINT is a very complex discipline, especially since the advent of the internet, big data, and advanced algorithms. Historically, information availability limited many open sources to newspapers, white papers, books, government records, and so on. Publications then were scarce. However, since the explosion of the internet and all its information sharing, OSINT has likewise exploded in capability. Not only is it just written information, but includes Imagery Intelligence (IMINT) as well. Again, before many of the social media platforms, their ubiquity, cultural changes of photography, and online sharing, the only sources for IMINT were surveillance planes and satellites. Now, with many people all over the world posting photographs of their possessions and activities, there is much more data to comb and analyze.

Due to the availability of data and the ease of creating algorithms, this is a capability that any adversary can own. Given, not all software is the same, because not all engineers are same. The accuracy and capabilities of each Adversary may differ, however, anyone who has access to the internet has some OSINT capabilities, which is nothing to scoff at.

Tradecraft helps operations and its symptoms hide in plain sight. Instead of trying to be invisible, the operation's indicators should be indistinguishable from normal activities. In a world where social media profiles and cell phones are ubiquitous, the Principal would be the odd one out if he did not have either. The Principal has more freedom in societies where the divide is 50/50, but that is not always the case. When the Principal needs social media and cell phones, he must be very careful with how he uses them. This is a fine line the Principal must balance for his specific circumstances.

Today, OSINT algorithms can pick out social media relationships even if the relationships are not explicit in the platform. That is one of the bragging point of some commercially available OSINT software: finding hidden relationships by analyzing them at the Nth tier, plus some other parameters, and they are quite good at spotting these hidden relationships.

When the Principal crafts a pattern for his natural behaviors, he must be consistent. If he adds customers and clients to social media, and claims a Resident as a customer, then the Principal should also add the Resident. If the Principal does not add anyone, then he shouldn't add any Residents.

The key benefit of OSINT is how well it finds patterns, which is based on the nature of how automated systems work. These systems execute algorithms over and over, like a pattern: a pattern to find patterns. The goal of tradecraft is to outsmart other humans, and in this case it is engineers who built the systems and the operators who use them.

There is quite a bit of information about OSINT and how big-data scientists are using it. If the Adversary would likely use this capability to find clandestine activities, the Principal should have a decent understanding of how it works. If the reader would like to explore this a bit further, there is a program called Maltego from Paterva.

Lastly, even if an automated system flags a Principal as suspicious, it does not mean the Adversary will mount up and hunt him down. It means the system has fit the Principal to a certain profile and someone should review or further investigate. This is where the Adversary begins to incorporate the other intelligence disciplines to dig deeper. They may start surveillance, hacking computers or cellphones, canvasing neighbors and so on. This is where the other parts of tradecraft come in. Therefore, it is crucial the Principal sanitizes both his physical and virtual possessions. If the Adversary starts probing, then they find nothing but the cover.

Designing a cover takes many steps. Developing effective covers relies on many factors. Which cover to select is more about what is available, not just fabricating something arbitrary. Which factors the Principal researches first to whittle down options will depend on the situation. If the Principal deploys to a free society, he may wish to start with the potential Residents and how he would approach them. If the Principal deploys to an oppressive region, he may wish to start with legitimate reasons for obtaining a visa.

The Principal must count all the clandestine activities he will conduct. The activities covered in this chapter include: counter-surveillance, caching, making contact, and paying Residents. Each one of these will need distinct reasons for doing each type of activity. Each activity needs certain behaviors at certain locations during certain schedules, which the cover must address.

Counter-surveillance often involves traveling large distances for longer periods of time, following a specified route. The cover must account for this whether it be a part of some job duty, errands, leisure, or some other reason. This must fit the natural patterns of the Principal in that it is common for him to do even when he is not performing counter-surveillance.

Caching often involves traveling to remote or desolate areas. These can be in either rural or urban environments, but the cover must incorporate why the Principal is alone for extended periods of time. If the Principal uses the excuse of nature photographer as a reason to get out to the woods with equipment, then he needs to be one. He must create reasons for getting into the profession, learn the needed skills, create a portfolio, and become an active member of the industry.

Making contact is heavily dependent on the Resident. The Personal circumstances, natural patterns, and the permissiveness of the environment will dictate where and when the Principal and Resident will first meet, what that initial connection was, and why they continue the relationship. Each contact venue has its own strengths and weaknesses, which the Principal will need to address with his cover.

Rural locations are one of the most secure environments to meet. It secludes a meeting from the rest of the population, but not everyone has a reason for such a presence. Rural contacts should have at least one other person to ensure security in case a third party gets too close to the meeting; however, a meeting does not need it. The Principal must research the community to find those who frequent the rural environments, and try to incorporate that into a cover. Often, people traveling between villages are those who meet in the rural.   Other activities include recreational site seeing, hunting, trapping, camping, and so on.

Urban locations are one of the least secure. Due to the nature of what an urban environment is: people are inherently a part of the landscape. Urban meetings need sites that are private, so members of the public do not accidentally stumble upon the meeting. Often these are hotel rooms, conference rooms, or some other establishment where the Principal can control the access.

The down side to urban sites are the points where the public transitions to the private: where nosy people pay particularly attention. Neighbors can see visitors enter and exit a home, and patrons can see people enter and exit hotel or conference rooms. Therefore, the area cannot be hostile toward the Principal or Resident. The cover needs to include why they would meet at these locations.

Vehicular meetings fall somewhere in between rural and urban in terms of security and feasibility. They do not seclude meetings as much rural areas, but are not as explicit as urban ones. Vehicular meetings have an element of access control, but the Principal and Resident are not completely out of view of the public. This meeting type makes up for the potential exposures by limiting the duration to any one person using mobility. The cover must include why the Principal and Resident met in a vehicle. This implies a deeper, more personal, or intimate relationship.

A Principal should not neglect proper payment, such as bonuses for the Resident or reimbursement for expenses. The Principal tries to use the relationship cover as a reason for conveyance. Eventually, that money will become known to those who know the Resident, and they will ask him where he obtained it. If the Principal chooses not to use a cover, or that the existing cover is not proper for such transactions, then he caches the money until the operation is complete. Furthermore, the Resident must have a plan to leave, so the Principal does not leave the Resident alone with money he cannot spend, lest risking compromise for past clandestine activities.

The Principal must research the culture to figure out what is common and proper for meetings and relationships. The Principal may have freedoms depending on what part of the world in which he is working as it pertains to the reason for his presence. In less developed countries, doctors may travel to patients, while in the more developed areas, patients may travel to doctors.

This leads into what the Principal can logically and securely claim as his cover. If the Principal is neither a doctor nor does not wish to become a doctor, then the Principal should not claim to be a doctor with Doctors Without Borders. Humanitarian efforts are common around the world, especially in the more oppressive regions. There has been a push to for entrepreneurs to start businesses in Asian countries like China, Philippines, Thailand, India, and Malaysia.

An important note about using these altruistic organizations and programs as covers: Avoid it. If the Principal does not keep his operation secure, he places others who are legitimately using these organizations at risk. If the Adversary begins to believe that others who claim membership to humanitarian efforts are also clandestine actors, then they may retaliate in kind. Many people already do use them as covers, even having not read this book.

Regardless, avoid using these benevolent organizations as cover to avoid harming others, or tainting the organization.

When considering who the Principal meets or what activities he conducts, he finds what would be socially acceptable for such a relationship. These relationships are not always based on professions. These can include personal relationships from shared hobbies or interests. The Principal should avoid inappropriate relationships at all costs, as those are rife with gossip.

Sometimes there may not be a good enough reason for a relationship, and the activities move into a more sensitive category requiring more sensitive tradecraft. In these instances, the Principal should have some form of cover even if it is flimsy, because human psychology has shown people do not always pay attention to the logic, they just want an answer to their question. However, the Principal should not completely rely on psychological tricks, and must rely on other tradecraft to avoid deploying a weak cover. This can include more secluded meetings or dead drops, and second-tier covers as a stop gap between the obvious lie and the clandestine truth.

A potentially complex actor is the government. First, the government does not always align with one side. Different branches of the government may split on which side they choose, or may not take any side at all, leaving the adversaries to deal with threatening activities themselves. Regardless of where the host government stands, the Principal must know where they do.

In terms of selecting a cover, the Principal must understand the three primary domestic functions of a government: legislative, executive, and judicial. Keep in mind that not all governments are as free and just as others, and even within a society, the agencies can differ between communities. Even in the United States, consider how the law differs with the use of drugs, or possession of firearms, and how those vary between each state and the federal government.

The Principal must figure out which laws pertain to his cover, especially if he is traveling to a foreign land. It is important the Principal researches this to ensure he does not try to claim a cover, be it profession or hobby, which authorities consider illegal or heavily regulated.

Enforcement of law is crucial, especially if the law enforcement has a probability of supporting the Adversary. In many of the harsher regions of the world, it is common for the government to deny any rights or privileges to citizens, let alone foreigners. There are still areas of the world where beating confessions out of a defendant is admissible in their version of court. This is where it is important for the Principal to understand the host nation's standards of proof, their investigative methodologies, and how they select their targets. The Principal must eliminate as many vulnerabilities as he can with a cover and tradecraft.

The Judiciary plays a vital role in terms of conviction and sentencing. The Principal should understand not just the punishments the laws include, but also if there are any biases to certain classes of people. Regarding those biases, it is important to know who in the judiciary will be deciding the verdict, be it a magistrate or a jury. The Principal should research past cases to find if there are any applicable patterns that he can alleviate with a cover.

After the Principal understands the cover considerations, he starts working on the concrete details. Public and human sources are going to be the Principal's best bet. When the Principal starts interacting with more people, especially more prominent people who have contacts in the target area, the Principal should consider deploying his cover. One of the most important parts of the cover is its genesis: the story of the "what" and "why" of the journey.

The Principal should avoid telling his real purpose, as gossip may travel unexpectedly. If the Principal is creating a cover from scratch, he should have some sort of life event catalyst. Even if he has had a strong urge to travel to a secluded and oppressive region to do whatever, his cover may involve something he has not considered before. For example, if becoming a business owner is the right cover, but the Principal has spent his life as a teacher, then he will need a reason for changing his life goals.

Often, people change their behaviors or lives because of some mental, physical, emotional, or spiritual catalyst. A couple of examples are: loss or gain of important relationships, intellectual epiphanies from life experiences, changes in health status, and so on. Regardless of how the Principal comes up with the reasons, they should satisfy more questions than raise.

The Principal must start sanitizing his life as soon as possible, so that it better matches his cover and allows for seasoning. The Principal should pay attention to those online accounts over which he has control. What the Principal specifically does to sanitize will be up to him. One possibility is for him to edit or remove only those posts and links that are explicit to his goals, or would otherwise contradict his cover: photographs, relationships with certain people, and so on.

Another possibility is to try to completely remove his accounts, and erase his online presence. The down side to this is how the internet works. Indexing is the storage of information in a database that helps with searches. Eventually, the data will be over written when it becomes too old, irrelevant, or for some other reason, but how long that takes is dependent on the organization that owns and keeps the systems and data. Some organizations are notorious for data persistence, where information may stay for years. How well the Principal can sanitize his online foot print should be a part of his risk versus gain assessment.

The Principal should have a reason for losing interest in his now public, yet soon to be clandestine goals, if applicable. If things change suddenly, he will need a stronger catalyst. If his behaviors change slowly, then simple explanations will suffice:

like the topic lost its novelty or life's other priorities are demanding attention. The key to much of this is knowing that humans are good at finding patterns and are sensitive to change. When changes in life happen, people begin to wonder why.

The Principal should incorporate a grace period between his catalysts. It would be obvious the moment he loses interest in the clandestine goals, that he starts talking about his cover goals. However, certain catalysts may suffice as a direct transition from actual goals to cover goals.

Sanitizing relationships are only necessary if the Principal cannot trust others will not intentionally or unwittingly betray him, or if the Adversary performs background checks involving interviews of associates. If people won't betray the Principal or the Adversary isn't savvy, then the Principal may only need a catalyst story. However, the Principal should still ensure he does not have a public presence online, which the Adversary could easily find.

Once the Principal selects a proper cover, he starts backstopping and seasoning it. These steps will depend on the target area and his personal circumstances. If he already has the occupation, position, status, hobbies, interests, and access to the area in which he will work, then he can start the next phases of the operation. However, if the Principal is missing one or more of the above, then he will need to do some preparation to solidify the cover.

If the Principal is going somewhere he has not yet been, he must get the paperwork in order. He will not likely go under the cover of a tourist, unless he is meeting the Resident in a permissive country outside the target area. In the beginning of an operation, the Principal should develop a cover that is more permanent. He fills out forms, submits to screenings, and jump through the bureaucratic hoops. This can vary depending on what the Principal claims as a cover. He must research, understand, and satisfy these requirements, while still being consistent. The Principal must not lie to get into the target area for ease, and then claim something else once there.

The Principal intends to be and do what he claims as legitimately as possible. Making fake IDs, printing out some business cards, and having some pocket litter is not ever enough. It may be enough in terms of a social engineering pretext and may even get the Principal past one obstacle, but a cover that is durable to conduct lasting operations needs to be significantly more legitimate and thorough. The Principal should seek the necessary credentials, licenses, visas, and so on. He must have legitimate contacts, associates, and references. He must do the work he claims, and build a legitimate reputation. A cover must be as real as possible. The only exception is the true motivation for doing it.

If the Principal uses actors, which is a riskier approach, he must ensure the stories between actors and himself are consistent. Handing out contact information of a reference without matching stories will surely move the Adversary from the probing phase to targeting phase. Just like any other cover, the stories must hold the right amount of detail, neither too much nor too little.

Once the Principal lays the foundation, he should spend some time fulfilling the role he claims. He should start frequenting the types of areas that he will use, and cultivating superficial, albeit legitimate relationships with the types of people he intends to recruit. He should give himself ample time to carry this out, so people begin to accept his behaviors as natural patterns. The Principal must not start clandestine activities when the public or Adversary are scrutinizing his presence. This is seasoning.

The Principal knows when seasoning is complete when people no longer look at him skeptically, or pay his presence too much attention; it is at the point where despite his foreigner status (if applicable), his is no longer anything of interest to talk about. The Principal balances his presence with his absence. People should feel equally comfortable with both. The actual ratio of presence to absence will depend on what locals consider normal for someone like the Principal.

The transition between seasoning the cover and setting up the clandestine relationships should be smooth, and hopefully unnoticeable. If the Principal executed the cover phase well, when he goes to approach his Residents, no casual observers will have anything to gossip about. The Principal is not performing any sensitive activities at this point, this is merely setting up the pretext from which the clandestine relationship will blossom.

The initial pretext is a crucial part of any relationship cover. This is the beginning of what will appear to be a natural and open relationship. This gives credibility to the shared cover story, which others will confirm through their testimony. The Principal should neither broadcast nor avoid using the cover, because overselling or underselling the cover may lead to compromise.

There are two ways of approaching the initial pretext: with or without an existing relationship. First is a mutually agreed upon pretext, where a clandestine relationship already exist, and the Principal and Resident try to set up a cover to legitimize it. The second is where no relationship exists yet, but one is desired.

The first approach may be problematic, because the parties already know each other: The Principal and Resident have a history, and now they are fabricating stories to fill the gap. Often, people will display guilty knowledge, which is knowing more than they should. Another issue is not accounting for all the potential questions an Adversary may ask, which will force both parties to fabricate the story on the fly. This is a problem, and is the number one reason a cover will fall apart. The Principal or Resident can remedy this by a second-tier cover, as most interviews and interrogations seek a confession. The Principal and Resident must discuss and rehearse the details of this second cover as well, because the investigators may wish to know more about these less-than-desirable activities. Again, the Principal ensures these covers satisfy more questions than they raise.

The second approach is more desirable. When the Principal is developing relationships, he runs the risk of exposing himself to the wrong person, but often that is an acceptable risk to take. The reason new relationships are more secure overall is because the cover existed since the beginning. The Principal maintains the cover by spending time during each meeting to further the relationship, because it is much easier to omit information than to fabricate it.

During the first contact, the Principal must develop a reason to meet the Resident. This applies to both preexisting and new relationships. People run into and interact with others all the time, but the cover needs to include what made the Principal and Resident stand out to each other, and why each party desires to continue the relationship. These are very important questions that investigators will seek to know, so the Principal makes it easy.

Action covers can be tricky. Where relationship and status covers are general, action covers address something specific. Status covers may explain why someone talks to certain types of people or frequents certain types of locations, but the action cover explains why the Principal is talking with a specific person, or is present at a specific location and time. Uses of action covers include the various stops during a surveillance detection route, loading or unloading a cache, or the purpose for meeting the Residents at that place and time.

The Principal has a limited number of cover choices he can deploy. He must approach actions and their dependencies from two sides: what is operationally secure, and what is logically proper. It matters not how operationally amazing a brothel may be, if it is completely inappropriate for either the Principal, Resident, or both to be there together, then it is off limits. The Principal can view this like a Venn diagram: Of all the locations that are secure, and all the locations that are proper, only those which are both are suitable.

Deploying a cover is only applicable while executing clandestine activities. The Principal does not need to plan and rehearse a story if he is not doing anything compromising. If the Principal is close friends with the Resident and a relationship exists outside of the operation, then only the clandestine acts need a cover. If the Principal decides to have dinner and just talk about family and life in general, there is nothing to conceal. If someone asks about non-clandestine acts, the parties tell the truth.

Of all the activities, the clandestine ones take up a very small part of the Principal's time and effort. There is a pseudo-joke: Two weeks of planning and preparation for a two-hour meeting. Most of the activities will relate to building or keeping covers. The Principal cannot spend all his time casing, running counter-surveillance, caching, and hold clandestine meetings. If he did, he would neglect keeping up appearances. Covers are important, because they keep people's suspicions at bay.

Counter-Surveillance is a crucial skill the Principal must hone to succeed in his endeavors. This chapter discusses both physical and technical surveillance methods at a very basic level, and then discusses counter-surveillance activities for each method to discover whether the Adversary is in a probing or targeting phase.

This chapter takes liberties assuming the reader is moderately familiar with physical surveillance. This chapter will offer a brief recap of basic surveillance methods, which establishes a basis for how counter-surveillance intends to exploit those surveillance methods. If the reader needs a basic understanding of surveillance, there are plenty of materials available in books and articles that explore surveillance extensively.

There are two primary approaches to surveillance: probing and targeting. Probing decides whether the Principal or Resident is a threat. These surveillance efforts include at least one surveillance operative who may not care if his target sees him. In fact, tail consciousness is an indicator that their target may have training thus implying some clandestine or nefarious motive. The most important behavior the Principal shows is ignorance, even if surveillance is obvious.

Targeted surveillance uses robust and professional surveillance teams, if available. This chapter discusses this type of surveillance, because the Principal can apply the same methods and techniques of countering larger, well-organized surveillance to smaller, less effective ones.

The Adversary has surveillance triggers, which are events that prompt the Adversary to begin surveillance. These may include an informant, another surveillance operation, or OSINT, and such triggers can fire at any time. Most triggers happen after the Resident performs some task to get information or materials.

To a lesser extent, the Principal may attract surveillance when contacting a Resident, loading or unloading caches, or reconnoitering a location that is important to the Adversary. Therefore, the Principal should conduct surveillance detection before and after any sensitive activities, so he is not leading the Adversary to any other clandestine activities or his cover life.

Foremost, the only purpose of counter-surveillance is to find the presence of surveillance in a way that does not show an attempt at surveillance detection. Counter-surveillance is not trying to lose surveillance by performing sneaky activities, running lights, or any other non-sense. If the Principal recognizes surveillance, he simply cancels the planned activities, and continues about his cover life. Nothing more.

Lastly, the threat of surveillance is not just from the Adversary, but may be from neutral or even friendly elements. Witnessing clandestine activities by anyone other than the intended participants may compromise the operation, which makes counter-surveillance activities a high priority for the Principal. In an ideal world, friendlies would leave the Principal's operations alone, or at least put in the same effort to safeguard the current Principal or Resident(s), so no one gets hurt; but alas, we do not live in such a world. Greedy or ignorant Principals from other organizations may intercept a Resident, and because of their lack of understanding or context, may place other lives or the operation in danger.

A key part to surveillance is exposure. Too much exposure and the target becomes witting. This is also what surveillance techniques seek to minimize. The two elements to exposure in the context of surveillance are: contrast and duration. To mitigate overexposure, surveillance relies on concealment or blending with the surroundings, so the target disregards the surveillance presence. Concealment tries to limit the surveillance's contrast, affording a longer duration.

The human mind is constantly trying to conserve resources, so it will disregard objects that fit an ordinary signature. Camouflage contributes to the success of surveillance by making its elements appear indistinguishable; however, the longer any element stays in the view of a target, the more the target will distinguish the finer details.

The four types of terrain are: urban, rural, suburban, and semi-rural. Each are characterized by the prominence and purpose of man-made features. Urban is heavily laden with man-made features to support various human activities and behaviors, like industrial, commercial, and residential. Human presence is prominent in urban environments. Suburban is a limited form of urban, often restricted to residential housing and limited commercial areas. In suburban areas, human activity, not its presence, is noticeably less than urban areas.

The lack of man-made features characterizes rural environments, and human presence is scarce. Semi-rural are those areas that are mostly rural, except there is some buildup of infrastructure to support outlying urban developments or human activities. This includes power and communication lines, highways, camp sites, trails and so on. Human presence in semi-rural areas is significantly more than rural, but much less than urban or suburban.

Aerial surveillance has expanded in recent years, especially in war torn regions of the world. The advent of unmanned vehicles has reduced the operating costs of fuel and size, which its recent proliferation by many of the world's military and governments show. The practice of its deployment is trying to work its way into more developed regions despite push back from citizenry. Two more reasons for a lack of wide spread adoption is current air traffic and platform reliability issues. In more authoritarian regions, aerial platforms continue to grow, as safety concerns are low, they are often no-fly zones, and citizens do not have a strong voice.

Aerial surveillance capitalizes on some of the benefits of distance over concealment. Unless the platform is too close and mimicking the target's movements, the target will stay oblivious to the platform. Aerial platforms offer the greatest advantage in the rural environment, as it offers the greatest command over great distances. However, these systems are still quite expensive compared to ground surveillance, so the Adversary may not deploy them unless justified and available.

Countering aerial surveillance is a matter of knowing whether it is a threat, and if so, paying attention to the skies and ensuring proper concealment over clandestine activities. At the time of this writing, most aerial platforms are not stealthy. They are loud and obvious. Their operators call these platforms "flying lawnmowers", because the sound they make even at distance.

One of the only ways to mitigate a target's awareness of aerial surveillance is by flying at higher altitudes. This presents two problems: aviation ceilings and sophisticated equipment. The higher the plane goes, the more the Adversary needs coordination with other planes. Furthermore, the platform needs special equipment to stabilize and see in higher detail. The latter contributes to higher procurement and operating costs. Most of the time, aerial surveillance flies at lower altitudes with smaller and less expensive platforms; fortunately, they are more obvious.

If a Principal sees this type of surveillance, he cancels all clandestine activities, especially in rural environments lacking overhead coverage or when relationships would be obvious, for example: only two people in the woods go to the same cave or building. However, if working in the urban environments, it is possible to make contact in public venues with dense populations. The Principal should use the right techniques described in the drops chapter.

Ground surveillance is the greatest threat to the Principal, and especially so in urban environments and developed societies.

For non-technical targets, it offers the most valuable information with the highest return on investment.

The standard surveillance headcount ranges from three to six elements. An element can either be a single operative on foot, or a vehicular team. Vehicle surveillance employs teams to separate the duties and offer logistical support in the event operatives dismount. Any fewer than three elements and the surveillance effort risks overexposure to the target as they rotate with scenery changes. Any more than six, it becomes a waste of resources and difficult to coordinate due to the lack of qualified operatives and high case load.

The actual number of operatives will depend on the available resources of the surveillance sponsor. If the Principal displays counter-surveillance training, then the Adversary may dedicate more resources to make it difficult for the Principal to spot the effort despite the greater troubles of coordination and expense.

Psychologically, the Principal sees his environment in a series of mental snapshots. The Principal cannot initially distinguish the surveillance operatives from the general population. At any given location, a person takes a snapshot and keeps it in short term memory. Subconsciously, the brain compares consecutive snapshots and if any similarities between geographically or socially distinct locations exist, the brain will bring the snapshots back into consciousness. Once the surveillance rotates through the team, the first elements are available again with less risk of overexposure.

Fixed surveillance, albeit simple and straight forward, is inherently difficult to spot. Therefore, progressive surveillance is difficult to see even when there is only one surveillance operative. Counter-surveillance relies on eliciting known responses from the surveillance effort; however, because fixed surveillance has little or no behaviors or movements, there is not much to elicit from those already in place. As for finding sloppy or intrusive fixed surveillance, people are naturally sensitive to loitering and other unnatural static behaviors.

Mobile surveillance is unique, because everything from the perspective of the Principal is changing: people, vehicles, and the landscape. Therefore, the surveillance must change with the surroundings to minimize the risk of overexposure. Surveillance techniques are a series of preplanned and rehearsed maneuvers designed to respond appropriately to a normal person's actions and behaviors.

Every mobile surveillance starts as fixed surveillance. The pickup is the moment the surveillance acquires the target and the target starts moving. Once both aspects of the pickup meet the above criteria (acquisition and movement), the mobile surveillance begins.

The follow is the duration of the mobile surveillance. This is the time where the surveillance effort pursues the target, and employs mobile surveillance techniques. After this, mobile surveillance returns to fixed surveillance, known as housing.

During the follow, the surveillance effort tries to position its operatives where they can best react to the Principal's actions, i.e. maintain coverage without drawing attention to their presence. Paralleling the Principal is most common. It allows the other elements to mostly hide from the Principal, yet observe him when he changes direction. The specific positions are: a) one element directly behind the Principal, known as command, b) one element on each side of the Principal, known as parallels, and c) one behind the command known as backup. This technique is known as the floating box. This box allows the surveillance to pass control between elements smoothly, instead of committing the command element with the Principal at most turns. This significantly reduces any given element's exposure to the Principal greatly.

Housing is a boxed pattern set up after the Principal finishes his travels, regardless of a temporary stop or a destination.

The housing box satisfies three conditions: the positions are at key vantage points where the surveillance can best see the Principal without moving; it expands far enough where the surveillance does not have to quickly react to the Principal's actions, yet close enough to prevent blind spots; and lastly to seamlessly join the follow.

The key to mobile surveillance is effectively changing the element in command to prevent overexposure. There are three scenarios where surveillance will rotate: during the pickup, direction changes, and during housing.

Regarding the pickup and housing, people are most sensitive at points of transition, and people cache these memory snapshots longer than others. Suspicions always rise when others appear to react to a person's behaviors, like leaving home, work, or getting out of a vehicle.

Not every change in direction may elicit a change in command. It is common while traveling in a crowd to have a few people with which to turn. To capitalize on this, and to save personnel resources, the command element may commit to a few turns before rotation; however, too many consecutive commits is obvious to even the most oblivious people. For surveillance, the limit is usually three turns. Any more and the surveillance risks overexposure.

The "ABC" or "street" dance is the term of the maneuver for changing command during the follow. In the traditional floating box, there are two elements behind the target and two elements paralleling. When the target turns, the elements shuffle in a way that allows them to realign around the target without any of them committing to the same turn. For each turn, the command and backup transition to the parallel positions, and the parallel positions transition to command and backup. Which parallel element becomes what, depends on which direction the target turns. Execution is rarely so graceful, as traffic and signals are not always conducive to a perfectly execution.

The next two terms are special and uncommon maneuvers.

Cheating is when vehicular surveillance is ahead of the target. The term derives from the passive nature of surveillance, because it reacts to the target. If an element is ahead of a target, and the target decides to make another turn, the element cannot follow the target without being obvious or reckless. Targets rarely suspect surveillance from the front.

Waterfall, performed during foot surveillance, is when the effort ferries operatives in front of the target and then pass in the oppose direction. While this significantly increases the rotation and frequency of when the target can see the team, the target is much less likely to suspect surveillance not only from the font, but traveling in the opposite direction.

Detecting ground surveillance capitalizes on the fundamental surveillance maneuvers mentioned above by specifically eliciting these behaviors, and then spotting a person or vehicle multiple times. The Principal keeps in mind that anyone could be surveillance, but not everyone is.

Through the process of elimination, the Principal whittles down potential surveillance. The Principal suspects those people or vehicles that remain during this detection process. The next phase is confirming suspicions through multiple sightings.

The Principal performs this process through predefined and previously cased routes and stops. The routes incorporate specific places and behaviors to which surveillance must react, while keeping an air of innocence and natural behaviors. The goal is to forcibly rotate the surveillance elements and spot at least one element multiple times. There are two criteria for multiple sightings to be legitimate: geographically and chronologically distinct.

The Principal should expect to see the same people if he stays in the same geographic area in a short amount of time.

However, as he gets further away from an area or is traveling greater durations, multiple sighting should become rarer, and thus suspicious. Upon suspicion, the Principal cancels all planned activities and tries confirmation: a third sighting of the same person, or a second sighting of a second person.

Confirmation also raises the risk of compromise. Surveillance detection is a well-known activity only performed by those who conduct clandestine acts. Doing more surveillance detection could confirm the Adversary's suspicions, which may force the Principal to abandon his operational goals.

For example, if the Principal plans a two-hour route, he should abort the remainder of the route if he suspects and confirms surveillance after 45 minutes. Whether the Principal ceases further surveillance detection after the second sighting will be up to him, but he must not fall prey to paranoia.

The Principal conducts surveillance detection activities either in a vehicle or on foot. The Principal should incorporate as many techniques without being obvious. If he has a vehicle, he should include both vehicular and pedestrian legs, ranging between three to five legs and stops for each. If the Principal does not have a vehicle, then his circumstances limit him to foot routes, and he should increase the number of legs and stops.

The Principal considers the use of public transportation as on-foot, as the Principal can control neither the route nor the access to the vehicle, and the Principal cannot consider strangers boarding with him to be suspicious on its own. The use of public transportation is optional. The Principal considers taxis as private transportation, and thus vehicular, when completing legs of a route.

The goal of a provocative phase is to confirm the absence of surveillance; however, the provocative phase is not completely reliable, because it is impossible to prove the lack of existence. It assumes that the Adversary would make itself known if forced into a decision to either lose the Principal or prevent a clandestine act.

It is therefore optional. The Principal may use a provocative phase as a last resort before conducting the most sensitive of activities.

Vehicular legs focus more on eliciting surveillance behaviors through the routes between stops, instead of the stops themselves. Public roads and parking areas limit vehicle movements and locations. Vehicles are easier to abstract than people, because of the lower amount of unique characteristics (make, model, generation, and color) . This makes it easier to keep track of vehicles while driving than keeping track of people on foot.

When building the vehicular routes, the Principal selects stops with at least three logical and natural turns between them. Any fewer turns risks elements not rotating during the leg. Adding unnatural turns is known as stair-stepping, which is a provocative maneuver. The Principal should avoid using them during the beginning routes. Any turns made within the housing box will not elicit behaviors, so the Principal must break the box before counting a turn as meaningful.

Route paths should never cross. The overall route should have a natural flow. This includes circular, snaking, or linear throughout or between distinct regions. The Principal should order the stops in such a way that he conserves both time and effort by minimizing the mileage, but does not neglect the turn requirement.

From the perspective of the Principal, there are times where the surveillance effort must react to changes in the environment. These include collapsing-fanning, changes in proximity, and out of place.

The concept of paralleling in the floating box has a flaw: it relies on roads that parallel the target's path; however, natural features and civil design prevents perfect uniformity. When surveillance comes across these obstacles, they collapse behind one another through the obstacle before fanning back out and getting into the box position.

There are two benefits to forcing this collapse and fanning behavior: it allows for observation and it forces the paralleling elements to travel greater distances, potential hindering coverage. There are two obstacles that force a collapse: corridors and choke points.

Corridors are roads or paths that have no paralleling. The Principal does this by incorporating routes with differences in speed over distance, natural obstructions, or a lack of infrastructure. Highways are a corridor because vehicles are free to travel at significantly greater speeds than corresponding side roads. Any attempt to drive at highways speeds on a side road is both obvious and dangerous. Naturally obstructed roads follow waterways, bodies of water, mountains, or cliffs. Roads through rural areas are examples of lacking infrastructure. The surveillance effort must travel along the same route as the Principal though these obstacles, thus granting him an observation opportunity.

Choke points are momentary corridors across some obstacle. The most prominent examples of choke points are bridges and tunnels. Often, the Principal will see a momentary collapse through the choke point followed by an immediate fanning.

The Principal may force surveillance to change proximity by entering traffic obstacles where they would need to close the gap to stay in command. Examples include: construction zones, busy roads during rush hour, and areas with heavy traffic control. The surveillance effort will try to get closer during these areas. Conversely, on open roads or freeways, surveillance may drop back and hide among other vehicles. By switching between these dense and sparse areas, the Principal may force the surveillance to react accordingly.

The Principal may quickly drop non-surveillance vehicles by changing the venue, as it is uncommon for people to travel between such distinct areas. Going through distinctly zoned areas, like residential, commercial, and industrial, or demographically specific areas will strip away most, if not all, non-threats. Spotting the same people or vehicles in unrelated venues is a strong indicator of surveillance.

The Principal should incorporate at least one of these elicitation techniques into each of his legs beyond the three-turn requirement. This will allow for greatest solicitation of the surveillance behaviors. The legs must be so logical, it does not appear the Principal is running surveillance detection. This means he should not go out of his way to incorporate these elements; rather, these elements should be logical to the Principal's route and plans.

When the Principal executes the legs, he must never break the laws, especially if the Adversary is working with law enforcement. If he does, he cannot be certain the ensuing stop, questions, and searches relate to his clandestine activities. Also, behaving so may bring him to the Adversary's attention if he was not before. The Principal should drive like eighty percent of the other drivers: Neither in the top nor bottom 10% in terms of speed and behavior.

When whittling down potential surveillance, the Principal should not try to memorize every vehicle in detail to compare later, as that is near impossible for everyone except savants. Instead, the Principal allows his mind to abstract the details of those in proximity at planned turns and obstacles. He thinks in terms of vehicle size, type, and color, and then abstract the occupants in terms of gender, complexion, attire, style, and frame. This allows him to remember more detail to compare later.

Any given leg should expose at least three surveillance vehicles at a time: observation post at the beginning of a leg, at least one during the follow, and an observation post at the destination. After three legs, the surveillance should have transitioned about nine times.

The Principal can disregard certain vehicles and suspect others via turns. At any given intersection, barring any upcoming corridors or choke points, the Principal can assume vehicles traveling in a different direction are not surveillance. The Principal must pay attention to those who turn with him (potential committed turn), or turn to join him (potential rotation).

When the Principal crosses a bridge or enters a corridor, only a hand full of vehicles may collapse behind him, and fewer still will fan back out after the obstacle. When he changes the venue, only a few will follow. The Principal should note these vehicles.

When the Principal sees vehicles or people a second time, he should obtain a little more detail. Observing things like make, model, generation of vehicles, and distinguishing features of the occupants, like mannerisms, activities, and unique body and facial features. This is will make confirmation more reliable.

At the end of the second leg, most, if not all, of the surveillance team would have exposed themselves at some point. This leaves the third leg to do multiple second-sightings, or a third-sighting of one element.

The significance of the vehicular stops is to justify the legs. The Principal selects stops carefully to support logic in cover and elicit surveillance. When selecting proper stops and legs, the Principal ensures they meet both criteria. If a stop or leg does not offer logic and elicitation, the Principal does not use it.

The stop should lure a surveillance element to enter. This involves a couple of key points: the stop should not be readily observable from outside, and should appear in some way that the Principal could perform a clandestine act. These key points entice the surveillance to enter with the Principal to keep command. This can be most sites, as clandestine acts include brush passes, brief encounters, dead drops, caches, and so on.

Each stop should last long enough for the surveillance to house and dispatch a dismount to enter the stop with the Principal; however, the stop should be short enough that the Principal leaves as the dismount enters, and just as the housing begins to take shape. The theory is it will cause the surveillance elements to scramble to regain command. This may not guaranty a desired response from a well-rehearsed team, but the opportunity may still present itself.

The stop should allow for the Principal a decent command of both inside and outside the site. He should assess both those who enter and the activities outside. When casing locations, the Principal should think like surveillance and find the areas where he would put a surveillance element. That way if an element is in that position, it is potential confirmation.

Each stop along a route should offer different products or services from the other stops. This is from the stand point of an action cover. It is illogical to go to several convenience stores, as one should satisfy what the Principal would need. The stops must fit the Principal's natural patterns and behaviors. If he does not smoke, he should not enter a tobacco shop.

When using the stop, the Principal should behave like any other normal patron. He must not make observation of these areas obvious, as that will confirm the surveillance's suspicions. The Principal must follow through with the cover activity. If he appears to talk to someone or buy something, he must not get impatient and leave, because the timing was a bit off. The cover takes precedence.

The number one rule for foot routes is to act and behave explicitly as it relates to the cover. Surveillance will not give the Principal a chance to explain himself. Behaviors that raise more questions will lead to more surveillance and dedicated resources.

Instead of eliciting behaviors during the legs, foot routes elicit behaviors at the stops. In vehicles, the Principal has mirrors and surveillance expects him to use them to a certain extent. Vehicles stand out more, because they are larger and it is normal for drivers to look around. The Principal does not have these luxuries on foot. Furthermore, people on foot are freer in their movements; they can be in more places and are more difficult to spot without obviously looking around.

Operatives on foot can and often are in positions ahead of the Principal. There may be one operative following him on the street, but the surveillance can position paralleling operatives at subsequent intersections in case the Principal attempts clandestine acts immediately after turning. While it is more difficult for vehicular surveillance to get ahead due to the limiting nature of traffic and streets, these restrictions do not apply to operatives on foot.

To counter these disadvantages, detection routes build in elements that allow the Principal to detect surveillance based on cover stops. The Principal first tries to force the surveillance to deploy dismounts. If he enters an area, but the surveillance can see his actions without moving, then the Principal may not see the surveillance. The Principal can use locations that: a) obstructs observation from vehicles, b) is difficult for surveillance to cover all entrances and exits, c) aid the Principal in losing command, and d) is conducive to a clandestine act.

These locations should be tight, remote, or heavily trafficked areas like: bazaars, markets, malls, piers, town or city centers, recreational or amusement parks, and so on. Once the Principal arrives to an area, he will do so in a vehicle, be it private, or public. The surveillance effort will set up housing around that point of transition if it is how the Principal will leave. This is either where he parked his vehicle or a public transportation stop. The Principal must travel on foot beyond the limits of this housing box. This forces the surveillance to deploy dismounts.

The Principal selects stops that have varying degrees of purpose. The goal here is to take the surveillance team out of their comfort zone of generality or ambiguity. If he goes into special purpose locations, especially those with helpful staff or social patrons, the Principal may see stumbling or distraction as the operative tries to look natural while performing his job. His mistake is not a guaranty, but the situation presents a potential opportunity. The more operatives used, the higher the chance an operative will make a novice mistake. The fewer operatives used, the more likely the Principal will spot the same operative multiple times.

The Principal may consider using stops that organize around a specific activity. If he goes to a social gathering, like a hobbyist get-together, business networking meeting, or some athletic meet, surveillance will stand out if not prepared. However, this is no guaranty, because professional surveillance researches, and knows what to expect from the Principal, but it may present a potential opportunity. The Principal avoids using stops which are outside his natural patterns.

As mentioned before, the use of public transportation is more akin to foot than vehicular, primarily because surveillance can board with the Principal and see his activities within. Think of this as a cover stop that takes the Principal to different areas. While it may be tempting to select a seat with command over the rest of the vehicle, surveillance may consider this a counter-surveillance flag. If the situation presents the Principal an opportunity to do so, then he may capitalize on it; otherwise, he selects a seat like anyone else.

If the surveillance can predict the Principal will board a bus, surveillance will try to have an operative onboard prior to him entering. They will also have others in position at stops ahead, so the command does not feel pressured to exit when the Principal does. As the Principal passes manned stops, surveillance will leap-frog to the bus's scheduled stops.

Subways, although not always available, are great, because surveillance cannot easily see the Principal within, thus forcing dismounts into the stations and onto the trains. Subways impede communications, and with their bidirectional nature, makes it harder to predict and react to the Principal's travels.

It is also good to travel between demographically distinct areas. Even though it makes the Principal stand out more, if it fits his cover it matters little. In response, the surveillance will either continue to rotate operatives as normal or limit only those proper operatives to continue the surveillance. Regardless, this gives the Principal more detection opportunities.

When it comes to execution, the Principal must have a logical plan and execute it properly. The focus is normal behaviors that have a byproduct of detection opportunities, not forcing detection opportunities and trying to mimic normal behaviors. If the Principal appears to shop, then he must shop, but builds in detection opportunities. If the situation becomes uncomfortable or deviates from his plan, the Principal should not hesitate to cancel activities.

The last phase is the provocative phase. This is where the Principal disregards the notion of trying to act normal in terms of logic, and employs anti-surveillance. The Principal must avoid drawing attention from casual passersby. The only people that would know he is acting illogically are surveillance. The lack of logic comes from the legs, as he is forcing multiple sightings in a brief time. The Principal should neither use this as the first phase nor if he suspects surveillance.

Stair-stepping is oscillating turns, where the Principal attempts to see operatives who have broken off and rejoined the follow on a parallel route. The idea is the Principal should not see the same normal persons at each intersection as he travels up and over through blocks.

Alternating driving speed along legs is another tactic that can yield opportunities for observation. While it is not advisable to drive over the speed limit, driving under or at the limit can be effective. The surveillance will either mimic the Principal's speeds or leap-frog. The key to spotting leap-frogging is knowing the patterns and behaviors of the other traffic and predict where the surveillance would pull off and rejoin the follow. If there is too much traffic, the Principal may find it impossible to track all vehicles that pass.

Stop-and-wait forces surveillance to house, and if the Principal just waits, the surveillance may struggle with their own cover activities. The only surveillance element guaranteed to be in the presence of the Principal is the command. Understanding that surveillance would rotate during housing aids in knowing which people to watch. The Principal can then assess for any illogical behaviors. The Principal considers using residential and industrial areas for this activity, as it does not give surveillance many options for behavior. The more desolate the area, the easier it is for the Principal to predict potential observation posts. The opportunity is checking these locations for potential surveillance as the Principal leaves the stop.

If the Principal executes the provocative phase under surveillance, it confirms the Adversary's suspicions. The Adversary may arrest or question the Principal on the spot, or break off and dedicate more resources later. If the Principal finds surveillance during the provocative phase, he should seriously consider ceasing all future activities and go home.

When the Principal offers counter-surveillance support to the Resident, he will do so at an observation post at a stop. The observation post adds another requirement for selecting proper stops. From the observation post, the Principal must be able to see anyone arriving to the area and the entrance to the stop. The Principal looks for the same behaviors and characteristics as above, with the exception the Principal is not the surveillance target.

The Principal should be able to see in this order: the Resident's arrival, followed by potential surveillance arrival and boxing behaviors, then the Resident's departure, and the surveillance pickup. These behaviors become obvious to someone who can see the area at a macro level. Professional surveillance teams are very much aware of this potential support, but they cannot mask all their behaviors.

Supported counter-surveillance activities do not need the same number of legs as unsupported. If the Principal obtains good command over the area and can easily see people's behaviors, then he can assess any surveillance presence or lack thereof. However, increasing legs and stops to confirm suspicions increases the opportunities, and therefore confidence in the counter-surveillance assessment.

Logic would stand that the Principal cannot leave after the Resident and get to the next stop quicker without arousing suspicions or breaking the law. This is true, because the Resident should take the most direct and logical route. If the Principal uses multiple stops, he must include timing stops for the Resident, which allows the Principal to set up before the Resident arrives.

Countering cellular interception is the last topic of this chapter. There are three general attack vectors that the Adversary could use to collect intelligence: software, base station, and backbone. None of these attack vectors are outside the realm of possibilities of any adversary, and each have their strengths and weaknesses.

Software is the simplest and least expensive way to start technical surveillance of a target, the proof is in the available applications to install on smart phones. This type of software only needs an external server to receive the data the software sends. It can access the camera, microphone, and GPS antenna and feed that information without the target knowing.

Software is also the easiest to detect, not necessarily with a malicious software scan, but because it relies completely on the device's resources. Using the camera, microphone, antennas, and the processor to collect data means that the battery will drain, data usage increases, and less available memory to run applications. If the Principal sets up a controlled network, he can see the data packets that the phone sends, and then find the server it is going to. However, the Adversary may limit collection to when there is a strong probability the Principal or Resident will do something compromising or sensitive.

Planned obsolescence of consumer electronics may have the Principal chasing ghosts. Just because his phone dies quicker or applications run slower, does not mean the Adversary infected his device with malicious software. It just might mean that his battery is dying or the software updates are taking their toll. Although, if the Principal's data usage goes up along with these, he may wish to stop all compromising activities and consider a network analyzer.

Obtaining a malicious base station is just a matter of combining the proper radio equipment with the proper open source software. With as little as $3,000 anyone with technical ability can intercept cellular communications.

The strengths of using a tower include the Adversary does not have to write the software to fit the handset, and the surveillance can continue to intercept communications as the target switches phones. However, this depends on whether the Adversary can get the target's phone on its network. Towers also have a direct link to the phone through the command channel, which allows the towers to force-update software or firmware on the phones, thus pushing malicious software for intelligence gathering and reducing the use of towers.

There are two ways of using this capability: either have a listening station that gathers all cellular communications in an area, or a mobile station to track a specific target on the move. However, due to the nature of how cellular communications work, and the automated process between phones and towers, the Principal, armed with a smart phone and open source software, can confidently spot the Adversary and any malicious equipment it uses.

Each tower must have an identity and broadcast it for the phones to connect. Furthermore, these identities cannot conflict with other towers in range; therefore, the Principal can map each tower. The Principal should spend some time tracking these towers, and noting their IDs and locations, so he can spot discrepancies during counter-surveillance.

Phones choose the towers to which they connect. This is based on a combination of signal strength and signal-to-noise ratio. Commercial towers are not only "louder", but clearer. Just increasing the signals output will not suffice as the noise increases too. The best way for malicious towers to overcome legitimate ones is by being closer to its target.

These malicious mobile towers, which must keep a certain proximity to its target to "win" the connection, are susceptible to discovery with special software available on smart phones. This software is known as Cellular Network Analyzers. This allows users to learn the tower ID, signal strength, and signal to noise ratio.

The Principal's job is to find the towers in an area or along a route, and record this information. If the Principal notices deviations from his records, he should cancel planned activities.

There are places in the world where infrastructure is not robust, and there are very few, even as little as one base station for a village or town. In such places, there is a significant possibility that the Adversary has access to these base stations, and no amount of analysis will detect it.

Lastly, the Adversary may access the telecommunications backbone. This means that the Adversary can gather information about the device remotely, as service providers pass this information between them. This vulnerability exists within the ubiquitous Signaling System Seven (SS7). The next iteration is SIGTRAN, which combines the SS7 technology with IP technology. To take advantage of SS7, or SIGTRAN, the Adversary needs access to the Public Switched Telephone Network

(PSTN), or whatever network the service providers may use for SIGTRAN.

This backbone vector allows much surveillance on a target without being anywhere near it. Someone in a foreign nation can track the Principal's or Resident's location, even without GPS, listen to active calls, read texts, reroute calls, and charge accounts. All the Adversary needs is a telephone number, which is easy enough to obtain.

This attack vector cannot collect on communications over the internet. While the vulnerability allows to temporarily confirm applications on another phone, thus gaining access to the Principal's accounts, that is more of a store-and-forward function, not decrypting data packets sent over the data networks. This means that encrypted browser traffic or use of Tor is still secure despite having their own vulnerabilities.

Furthermore, the Adversary can only collect on known phone numbers. If the target switches phones, the Adversary cannot listen until it adds the new number to its target list. It is important the Principal keeps communications compartmentalized; if there is a breach in one communication network, then he should easily walk away from it knowing that it will not compromise other Residents.

The Principal should never communicate anything compromising over the phone. Whether it is audio, text, or data, the Principal must limit all communications. The exception is the use of signals or codes which the Principal must design to not appear obvious and should coincide well with the both parties' covers.

For more research on these vulnerabilities, search terms include: Software Defined Radios, OpenBSD, OpenBTS, Signaling System 7, and IMSI Catcher. From there, the reader can fine tune his knowledge base and find his own vulnerabilities.

The main purpose of a cache is to separate the clandestine life from the cover life. The Principal sanitizes his cover life from anything compromising and caches those compromising things for safe keeping. To effectively plan a cache, the Principal must address: purpose, contents, duration, the Adversary, locals, packaging, transportation, and his cover.

The purpose of the cache affects its contents, location, packaging, and duration. Caches support a separation of concerns, so if the someone finds or destroys one cache, then the Principal will not lose other important contents. The cache must neither name the builder nor recipient, and should not hold fingerprints, items only accessible to the builder, hand writing, identifying documents, serialized items, and so on.

The three primary caching purposes include:

Medical caches, which the Principal used in anticipation of an activity risking bodily harm. These caches are in proximity to areas where he may need first-aid or critical field treatment, thus limiting transportation and potential exposure.

Escape or survival caches, which the Principal uses when the Adversary compromises his cover. The Principal deploys these caches in a chain to ease travel to sanctuary as a part of a ratline. The following chapter discusses ratlines.

Operational caches include several sub-categories. While the above are contingency caches used in the event operations do not go as planned, operational caches are integral to carrying out specific activities. Sub-categories include: communications (including phones or specialized software), administrative (storage devices, encrypted operating systems), and special equipment (anything needed to do a special task and does not fit within a cover).

The Principal must avoid contents holding identifiable biometric data, like photographs or fingerprints, and items registered to, licensed to, or subscribed by the Principal. An exception would be travel documents. If those are necessary, then the Principal may booby-trap the contents to destroys them if improperly opened, but does not harm the opener.

The Principal analyzes his requirements to incorporate everything he needs and exclude things he does not. The larger the cache, the more work. Expired contents can make the cache useless. Fragile contents need protection. Metal needs painting and separation to reduce the risk of corrosion.

The Principal must keep all things needed to carry out a specific activity together. He should limit the number of caches accessed, so he does not retrieve several caches to do basic activities. The exception is if certain items when paired together compromise an activity, like encryption ciphers and keys. If discovered together, the discovery compromises a network. The Principal should keep them close enough to access in one trip, but not close enough someone could discover them together.

The duration of a cache relates to its purpose. Medical and operational caches have an expectation of use at a known time, while survival caches lie in wait for an emergency. For planned use caches, its contents must stay usable from the time of packaging to probable recovery. The Principal should ensure that the items of the cache do not expire before he needs the cache. The Principal may need to wait before getting the contents and cache them when the expiry covers the required period.

Emergency caches need documentation and maintenance. It is unknown when the Principal may need the cache, so emplacement is sooner than later. The documentation lists the contents and their expiry, or needed maintenance schedule. Maintenance of a cache is retrieving the cache, and then replacing or performing maintenance on its contents.

The Principal should consider the activities and behaviors of the Adversary, so that the Adversary may not catch him in possession of such contraband. Considerations include: checkpoints and patrols. To minimize the risk of interacting with the Adversary, the Principal should source the contents within the area of the cache site. If that is not possible, then he should set up a ratline to bypass the checkpoints and patrols between the areas. Regardless, route and schedule choice will minimize the risks of coming across the Adversary.

The Principal should avoid the Adversary's areas of interest. These are areas the Adversary would find suitable to commandeer, attack, develop, or guard. Schools, stadiums, abandoned buildings, critical infrastructure, like power lines, railways and stations, water ways, and so on, are historically significant during conflict. If used, the Principal may lose access to the cache.

Locals pose two threats if they discover a cache: they may take it or notify the Adversary. Locals of conflict areas tend to cache. Locals use caches to store and preserve valuables and weapons. The Principal should research and avoid areas frequented by treasure hunters. Armed with metal detectors or probes, these hobbyists are looking for items left behind or natural treasures.

Casual traffic is most threatening during emplacement and recovery. To mitigate this threat, the Principal selects routes and schedules that will avoid observation. The Principal selects sites that limit interaction with casual passersby and offers good observation posts with command of the area, so he can see any passersby well before they see him.

Packaging needs an outer container, which the Principal can fabricate or improvise, and wrapping material to protect the contents in the container. Not all materials are available for packaging, and some may be so valuable or scarce, it becomes cost prohibitive, like stainless steel or Kevlar.

How the Principal packages the cache will depend on the contents, the container, and the environment in which the Principal stores the cache. Metals, while durable, are susceptible to corrosion. Glass and electronics are brittle and need padding. Some items need oiling, and others kept dry. If the container is of low quality, then the Principal wraps the contents well to prevent damage.

Lastly, the Principal considers the contents' physical characteristics. He makes the cache as small and light as possible, and matches the construction materials and items available with the cached contents. This may take some ingenuity and creativity with certain items in an improvised container, or making due with limited materials.

Concealing the cache during transportation only protects the cache against routine searches. Routine searches are those with no specific target and the Adversary probes the public. If the area is prone to routine searches, the Principal should know what to expect. However, if the Adversary targets the Principal, then the search will compromise him. The Principal conceals the cache by either disguising it as something the Principal can explain with a cover or placing it somewhere to discourage the search.

Route choice helps avoid potential interactions with the Adversary. Casing gives the Principal information about the Adversary's presence, and when and where transportation is most secure. The Principal should record the Adversary's and local's natural patterns and behavioral exceptions, and plan around them.

With the above consideration, the Principal starts deciding on the concrete details of his cache. Having a clear idea of the type and use of the cache will lead to the caching method. After this, the next three criteria for a suitable cache site are: findability, accessibility, and concealability.

Findability is how well someone can find an emplaced cache. It is easy to select a location, but it can be exceedingly difficult to find it again. Sites need both permanent and prominent features for reference points. The Principal considers what may look prominent from one direction, may not be so from another, and what may look permanent may be seasonal. Not addressing these considerations will lead to not finding the location again.

Accessibility involves the ease of reaching the site. This may not apply for smaller and lighter caches, but is something to consider for heavier or larger ones. The site needs at least two separate routes into the area coming from different cardinal directions and separated by at least 90 degrees. It must also have a backup route to emplace or retrieve the cache. There should be an escape route to quickly leave the area, which does not need to accommodate the cache.

Concealability is how well the Principal can return the site to its natural appearance. It is impossible to return snow to its natural look and excess dirt from excavation needs disposal. Two options for excess earth is: scattering among bushes, or flushing in a stream. These features must be close enough to minimize time and movement during emplacement.

Map surveys are the first step in casing. They show obvious areas of interest, which allows the Principal to quickly decide areas of further interest and areas to avoid. This narrows the list of potential sites to only those most promising.

Area familiarization is taking note of the natural behaviors and patterns of a region through direct observation. This is the abstraction of an area to better understand the obstacles the Principal faces. Maps do not give complete details, such as demographics, local behaviors, law enforcement or adversarial presence, and so on. This allows the Principal to view things on the ground and correct outdated information on the map. Area familiarization allows the Principal to take a deeper look to figure out the suitability of the location, including both the actual site and the routes throughout the area.

More considerations include: population make-up, behaviors, and activities. The Principal must know what the locals are doing at the given time of any operational act. Sometimes a certain area can become disruptive and draw unnecessary attention, so the Principal avoids these activities. This is one of the reasons for alternate routes.

The Principal avoids people while transporting a cache on foot, and especially so with larger caches. The Principal notes any foot paths that may generate too much attention, be it noise or visible presence, and avoids them. He must select paths offering enough concealment and logic.

Escape routes allow for hasty getaways. They do not accommodate movement with the cache, and the Principal should not assess it to do so. This route plays to the Principal's strengths and mitigates his weaknesses. The purpose of the escape route is to increase distance and time from the Adversary without it spotting the Principal, so if the Principal does cross the Adversary again soon, it is under a different context not associated with caching.

The Principal should plan for contingencies, playing the what-if game along the potential routes. He must not let hypothetical situations distract him by compounding what-if scenarios. Rather, the Principal war-games along his routes, and decides what to do if faced with certain threats or obstacles along them. The Principal should physically go down these routes and detours to make sure they are suitable alternatives.

The Principal should have plausible covers for every route and every leg thereof. He should have a good cover for the final demarcation from and after his re-entry on a common path. Between demarcation and re-entry, the Principal is not likely to have a suitable cover for caching; however, the action covers surrounding the emplacement or recovery should be suitable.

Demarcation points are where the Principal leaves a common path to make his final leg to the cache site. This is often an illogical route; therefore, he must ensure that the demarcation is not observed. He must have some form of concealment from others who might be in the area as he leaves the path.

Re-entry points are like demarcation points, except it returns to a normal path from an illogical one. It is important to find a re-entry point that is non-observable as well. It should be different than the demarcation, and further along the trail or road in the same direction of travel.

The re-entry point should have an observation post where the Principal can ensure no one will see his entry back on the normal path. This observation post should offer a decent command of the area, but not so open that the others may see the Principal. The Principal should follow basic camouflage techniques.

The primary cache site is what the Principal finds to be the most suitable: the location the Principal will try to use. However, for any reason that site becomes unsuitable at the time of emplacement, the Principal must have an alternate site cased and ready to use.

When selecting an alternate site, it must satisfy two requirements: close enough to the primary where it does not involve any other routes, and is out of sight and sound of the primary. The idea is if someone else occupies the primary site, or the site has some sort of obstacle, the Principal can safely bypass it and emplace the cache at the alternate site without having to make an extra trip.

Reference points are permanent and prominent features, be it man-made or natural, which the Principal can use as way-points to guide him to the cache site. The permanence of a reference point is proportional to the cache's utility. Things like ribbons that mark boundaries may only last a couple of months before they deteriorate or disappear. This may be acceptable if the Principal only needs the cache for that period. The reference points need to be readily identifiable from many directions and is distinguishable from other similar features in the area. Prominence does not have to be uniquely visible, but a numbered object in a series of uniquely similar objects, for example: the fifth intersection of the trail and a creek.

There are two special reference points: initial reference point and final reference point. The initial reference is the closest prominent feature on any common map, like major intersections between roads, railways, rivers, and prominent buildings and monuments, like city halls, libraries, stadiums, cemeteries, schools and so on. The initial reference point starts the chain of reference points leading to the cache.

Each reference point should include a distance and cardinal direction to the next reference point. Exact distances are not important. The Principal uses these measurements to get in the general vicinity to start looking for the next reference point. Expect to be off by several feet or yards; therefore, it is crucial to have prominent and permanent features as references.

The Principal only needs reference points when changing direction or modes of travel. The Principal does not need a reference point to continue along an obvious path. The Principal minimizes the number of reference points to get to the cache site, to make it easy to remember. These reference points eventually lead to the final reference point.

Concealment caches often collocate with the final reference point, while burial caches are some distance and direction from the final reference point(s). The concealment cache should be obvious to see from the previous reference point.

All caching techniques share a few tasks, which include: scheduling, acquisition, packaging, transportation, location, emplacement, exfiltration, and recovery.

Scheduling is the first task and it aims to minimize the possession of potentially compromising items. After completing the casing and site choice, the Principal coordinates building and emplacing the cache with its contents to limit his possession of them. The Principal uses backwards planning to incorporate all the steps needed in the operation in a fluid manner.

Acquisition of materials, supplies, and equipment takes place once the Principal finishes scheduling. The Principal gets materials in order of least to most compromising to minimizes their possession. The last thing the Principal wants is to have compromising materials while he builds and tests the containers, or while he gets the other contents.

Packaging is a very detailed phase of caching and includes:

Inspection to make sure that all contents and items are in good, serviceable condition, and function as expected. An effective way to ensure this is to assemble the contents, conduct a functions check, then disassemble to a proper level and package them.

Cleaning items before final packaging. The Principal wears rubber or clean cotton gloves when handling and preparing the cleaned equipment. This prevents the bodily salts and oils from corroding metals and fingerprints from getting on the contents.

Drying the contents and the container, if applicable. There are three ways of drying: absorbent cloth, like microfiber or linen, heating in an oven at 110 degrees for at least three hours, or using a desiccant like silica gel, which is good to use regardless of drying method. The Principal ensures that the desiccant does not come into direct contact with metal items in the cache. The ratio of silica for storage is just under 1 lbs. per cubic foot of storage or 15 Kg per cubic meter. This will be enough even if the items are slightly damp.

Preserving ensures the contents do not deteriorate in storage. For metals, electronics, clothes, and fragile items, this means preventing corrosion, electrostatic discharge, mildew, and shock respectively.

Wrapping contents individually is one of the most important steps in caching, as it can offer the most forgiveness when other preparations fail. Therefore, the choice of the proper wrapping materials is crucial and has a few requirements: moisture proof, sealing, pliable, and tear or puncture resistant.

Wrapping, which the Principal can do in layers, especially if limited materials offer limited benefits. It is common for cached items to have an inner layer, which keeps the preservatives against the contents, removes air pockets around the item, and offers a significantly more durable outer layer. The outer layer may not be necessary if the Principal arranges the contents well, and the container or padding prevents contact. The following is a list of suitable materials and their properties:

Aluminum foil is one of the best inner wrappings, but it needs an outer later, because it tears easily. Aluminum foil is good at keeping moisture out and can form around the object. Aluminum foil is also good with adhesives, so it seals well.

Waxed paper is good for metals and wood, because the wax adds protection as it makes contact. The down side is it does not stick well with adhesives. It contours and allows for tight wrapping as an inner layer. These need a moisture proof and sealing outer layer as well, to keep moisture from working its way in.

Rubber sheets are both durable and water proof, and available with an adhesive backing. However, they do not fold, and cannot contour to items as well as other wrappings. Adhesive-backed sheets usually need a nonstick inner layer.

Waxed or oiled cloth are thicker and more resilient than its paper counterpart. The shipping industry used waxed cloth for decades. This makes a great outer layer, but might need a sealing inner layer.

Wax, by itself, can encase some items. Melting the wax and applying a coat over the items, especially woods and metals, may be enough when other materials are not available. This will get into all the joints, cracks, and folds well, and keep a water proof barrier.

Plastic wrap comes in several kinds: cling, shrink, and stretch. Each have their own characteristics. These are good for both inner and out wrapping, as they offer water proofing. It is important to note that cling wrap loses its adhesion when moisture touches it. These are also good when binding individually wrapped items together. While they do offer elasticity and relative strength, they easily puncture, so coupling this with a soft inner wrapping, or tougher outer wrapping can help alleviate this issue.

Once the Principal prepared all items for caching, he organizes and places them in the container. The Principal should fill gaps in the container as much as possible to remove air pockets. Using clothes that aid the recovery party also helps with shock absorption. The Principal separates items that should not come into contact, like heavy, metal objects and small, delicate or fragile equipment. The Principal packages the contents as if the container would leak, where the items least susceptible to water damage are on the bottom. Order contents where the most durable or heavy objects are on the bottom, and the lighter or fragile objects on top.

The container is the first line of defense from the environment and serves to keep the contents together. Burial containers must protect against moisture, shock, pressure, animals, and corrosion. Concealment caches must protect against moisture, shock, animals, and observation. There are two types of container construction: fabricated and improvised.

Fabricated containers are those built from raw materials. The most suitable container material is stainless steel. However, this needs much more tooling and equipment to build from scratch. If the Principal has the skills and equipment, then this is best. The

Principal can also use fiber-reinforced plastics, like fiberglass. These do not need as much specialized tooling and equipment, and the Principal can fabricate them without noise. Manufactured containers need attention to the openings, like the joints and seals. Some containers may need handles or straps, especially if larger or awkward.

Improvised containers are those made from already existing items and are repurposed for caching. These include paint cans, metal drums, PVC, ABS, or metal plumbing, or even glass jars. Because these are premade, there are limits to what the Principal can put in them. He should cater the contents to match the container, so that things do not rattle or bang around inside. Each of these items have strengths and weaknesses, and it will be up to the Principal to capitalize and mitigate accordingly.

The Principal tests the caches by submersing it in hot water and looks for bubbles. Hot water reveals container leaks better than colder water. If there are bubbles, he fixes the leak. If he cannot, then the Principal must find or fabricate another container.

There are three primary caching techniques: concealment, burial, and submersion. The book only discusses the first two in detail, as submersion needs much more planning, preparation, and technical ability.

Concealment caches hide in or among other natural or man-made features or objects. Common examples are: walls, floors, ceilings, culverts, sewers, wiring conduits, coniferous plants, hollowed trunks or logs, rock formations, caves, and so on. The principles of exposure and logic hold: The Principal does not cache in areas frequented by others who could discover the cache. Imagination is the only limit, if the Principal cases the location well, others will not find it.

The primary advantage for concealment caches from which other advantages derive is the ease of use. Concealment caches are the easiest and quickest form of caching, because the Principal simply places them in an already existing feature. The simplicity and ease of emplacement also means that the packaging is often less critical in terms of preservation, especially for indoor caches. Disguising the container in its surroundings is the focus of attention. Outdoor containers need the addition of water resistance in case of rain or snow. Concealment caching is quicker and easier; thus, the cover is more secure by not needing to explain behaviors, equipment, or soiled clothes.

The primary disadvantage is others can discover these caches more easily. Just as the Principal found the location suitable, others may too. The environment limits concealment caches to some feature. Places like abandoned or unfrequented locales can attract rummaging explorers. The Principal may lose access to indoor or private property caches, as they are susceptible to changes in ownership, repurposing, or damage.

The Principal uses concealment caches for items requiring quick or frequent access, which may justify less security. The Principal uses concealment caches for smaller contents relating to operations, such as communication (USB-bootable Linux distributions, phones, radios, signaling items), administration (reports, files, dossiers, money), and encryption (cipher programs, encryption keys). These caches are usually around the size of a pack of cigarettes or smaller.

The Principal avoids using his own, relative's, or friend's residences, vehicles, or work locations as cache sites. If the Adversary discovers the cache, they may suspect the Principal merely by association. The cache locations should be those to which anyone can access for plausible deniability.

The equipment needed to successfully cache depends on where and how the Principal is caching. The two methods of concealment caching are: among and within.

Concealment caches among other items or features need some sort of concealment device. The concealment device ensures that the cache is indistinguishable from other common items like: trash, rocks, or vegetation. If the Principal fabricates the container, then he makes it look like the other items. If improvising a container, then the Principal may need to insert it into a concealment device.

For small, natural-looking caches, the Principal should paint the container similar colors of the area, coat the outside of it in an adhesive, and attach items found in the area, like small rocks, dirt, and foliage. Lastly, the Principal must add something that makes the cache slightly distinguishable from the immediate surroundings. It should stand out for those looking for it, but not so much that it draws attention from those who are not.

For small, arbitrary-looking caches, the Principal looks for items in the area that are common and not often disturbed. He creates the concealment device to look like these items. The Principal ensures the cache is not in the open, but tucked away somewhere. For larger items, the Principal may create a concealment device from molding or sculpting material, like foams, fiberglass, and clay, which he can paint and texture to match that of the surroundings.

Emplacing the concealment cache is often straight forward. For those that hide among other features, the Principal puts it where others cannot easily see it, and walks away. For more exposed caches, the Principal may need to blend, so the cache is not in plain view; he nests it between other items. Examples include trash or foliage.

Burial caches are those emplaced in the earth. The Principal can cache in both urban and rural environments; however, the rural is more common, because it offers more seclusion from human activity. There are two types of burial caches: vertical and horizontal.

Vertical caches are the most common: the Principal buries it down into the ground, as opposed to the horizontal into a steep hillside or bank. Vertical caches are often more suitable, as horizontal caches are more prone to exposure through erosion, but if there is no suitable vertical cache site, then horizontal is the choice. A benefit to horizontal caches is they offer better drainage during heavy rainfall.

Just as concealment caches offer strengths and weaknesses, burial caches have their own. Where concealment caches lack in security, burial caches are secure for extended periods. The Earth conceals burial caches, so it is more accommodating for varying sizes and shapes of a cache. Burial caches can be most anywhere there is exposed ground, so the options are plenty.

There are several disadvantages and obstacles with burial caches: The containers must be significantly stronger, emplacement and recovery take much longer, higher risk of damage from pressures, animals, and corrosion, more difficult terrain, more equipment to emplace, and more difficult to conceal.

Burial caches have additional considerations. Drainage involves elevation and slope to prevent pooling. Ground cover is what and how the Principal must restore the scenery after emplacement and recover. Subterranean ground impacts excavation, so the Principal should avoid rocks, clay, sand, and deciduous trees, as their roots make digging difficult. Scenic restoration involves how the ground returns to its natural state.

Often, the Principal conceals small items, like communications or flash drives, and buries the larger items, like clothes, weapons, medical supplies, food, and so on. Caches should be no more than 30 lbs. and about the volume of a small travel bag or carry on. If the cached items exceed this size, then the Principal should separate them into different caches.

As mentioned earlier, burial caches need much more equipment. The tools needed are as follows: a two-foot probing rod, a measuring device resistant to stretching and distortion, digging equipment, ground sheets (one for topsoil, sod or ground cover, and another for subsoil), and a flashlight with a red lens to conserve night vision.

The Principal can find burial caches three ways: triangulation, distance-and-direction, and sight-projection. The Principal only needs to get in a vicinity that is as large as the cache itself. The Principal tries to be as exact as possible, because errors may compound resulting in failure to pinpoint the cache.

Triangulation: With two reference points, the Principal can either use the distance between these points, or an arbitrary measurement from them. The former is known as equilateral triangulation and the latter is isosceles triangulation. The Principal performs this by using a fixed point on each of the reference points and measures the distance out. The point is the intersection between those two distances.

Distance-and-direction: The Principal shoots an azimuth from the reference point and travels in that direction a specified distance. It is best to use a compass that has degrees on it, rather than a general cardinal direction. The Principal should perform this within 10 yards, as accuracy diminishes with longer distances.

Sight-projection: The Principal aligns two reference points, and projects a line on the ground. The Principal may use one reference point if it has a sufficiently long and flat side. Then the Principal measures from the nearest reference point to find the cache along that projected line. This is best suited for distances less than 50 yards.

Marking a cache may be proper during emplacement and recovery operations. The Principal finds the cache during the day, and marks it for easier recovery at night. This can offer a suitable setup for a cover, like losing something desperately need. A general rule for markers is they blend well with the environment, but obvious to those looking for it.

Excavation has three considerations: size, shoring, and timing.

Size: The size of the hole should only be as large as needed to effectively emplace the cache. It will be wider than the container, because the Principal must dig down 18 inches further than the height of the container. The Principal may need to dig outwards to give him room to work.

Shoring: Depending on the type of ground in which the Principal is digging, he may need to dig out, and shore the hole to keep earth from constantly falling in, like sand or lose dirt.

Timing: The Principal gives himself ample time to finish digging and filling the hole. Experience is the only way to accurately figure out how much time the Principal needs.

When filling the hole, the Principal starts with the subsoil from the right ground sheet, making sure to compact the dirt as he fills. He replaces the top soil once he gets to the depth from which he removed it. The Principal must find a place to dispose of extra soil. Creeks or rivers are best, but the Principal may need to scatter it in a few different areas. The Principal conceals the site by spreading the ground cover to return it to an untouched appearance.

The Principal must not leave anything behind outside of the cache. The Principal makes a check list of equipment, and uses the list to account for everything he brought. The Principal may return to the site the following day to make sure he left nothing behind and that the cache appears as it should.

When recovering the cache, the Principal must consider how he will fill the cavity once he recovers the contents. If the Principal built the container appropriately, the Principal may leave the container and place the contents in a backpack. Otherwise, he can use surrounding materials or bring something to fill the cavity. Regardless, he should plan this before recovery. The rest of the recovery is much like emplacement.

The only way to become good at caching is to practice. Set up exercises with friends or like-minded people, and test the different methods, construction materials, and techniques. Do not cache valuables until finding a reliable way to cache. First, test it for a week, then a month, then six months, then a year. See how it performs when enduring all the seasons. For more information on caching operations reference Technical Circular 31-29: Special Forces Caching Techniques.

A ratline gets the Principal from a place of hostility to sanctuary. While the more common ratline examples of WWII and the Cold War involved grandiose circumstances, the Principal's ratline is on a much smaller scale. The Principal is not necessarily trying to cross the globe to get away from a coalition of adversarial nations; rather, he is trying to get to a place where a small and limited adversary cannot reach. If the Principal is trying to get away from a contemporary Axis Powers, he should reconsider his goals. There is no sanctuary for those who wanted internationally. For examples, look to Adolf Eichmann and Osama bin Laden.

If the Principal needs a ratline, then he is working in a small, poor, or rural country, or some desolate subsection thereof. The Adversary is often a disorganized, albeit violent, group of criminals or extremists. If the government is cooperating with the Adversary, due to corruption, a neighboring country may be the Principal's sanctuary. However, most of the time the Principal will make his way out of the Adversary's territory to a friendly or neutral one.

It is important to note that when it comes to diplomacy, an embassy will not sacrifice its relationship with the host nation to protect a citizen who broke local laws or customs. If the Principal offends the host nation and seek asylum in his embassy, regardless of how corrupt host nation is, the embassy may turn him over upon request. However, a part of the job of an embassy is to offer information and resources to citizens abroad. If the Principal coordinates the ratline well, he can get the help he needs from the embassy and get out of a country before the Adversary has a time to invoke diplomatic agreements.

Once back home, the government would be hard pressed to extradite the Principal for the violations the intended audience of this book would perform. For example, the United States. should neither extradite its citizens for proselytizing in a Muslim nation nor exposing the human atrocities of an oppressive regime. If the Adversary catches the Principal in the act, he should not expect some Tier-1 unit to come to his rescue; however, once he is home, he should not worry the State Department will send him back for capital punishment.

If the Principal executes a ratline, it is because he received an early warning for imminence of hostility from a Resident, embassy, or local news. Often, the Principal's actions do not lead to compromise; rather, local behaviors change in such a way mobs or incited extremists target people who stand for what they hate, like western foreigners. Unfortunately, these threats are not exclusive to just clandestine actors, anyone who is of the wrong demographic at the wrong place and time would be in danger.

If the Principal discovers a compromised operation and the Principal needs to get from the target area to sanctuary, then a ratline could help. The security during the ratline depends upon hostiles not recognizing or spotting the Principal during movement. A ratline seeks to avoid any potential points of encounter by devising routes around them. If the Adversary does not know exactly where the Principal is, where he is going, how he is getting there, or tracks him faster than he travels, then a ratline may help the Principal evade the Adversary.

A ratline consists of a series of legs, stops, and caches. Legs get the Principal closer to sanctuary, stops aid in schedule coordination between movements, and caches supply whatever the Principal needs to successfully complete the leg. The Adversary will not have enough personnel to support a perfect presence throughout the target area. With proper casing and understanding of the Adversary's presence, the Principal can capitalize on these gaps through which his routes can slip.

Unfortunately, many of these gaps are often in difficult terrain, and depending on the part of the world in which the

Principal works, some seasons make certain potential routes impassible. The Principal plans for this and cases different routes for different circumstances.

There are four environments which a ratline may traverse: aerial, maritime, urban, and rural. Each have their own strengths and weaknesses, as well as planning and execution considerations. There are always urban and rural components to a ratline; however, aerial or maritime components will heavily depend on the region, the operation, and available support.

How special operations forces infiltrate and exfiltrate a denied area are examples of ratlines, albeit not in the conventional sense nor in a sense many readers of this book may enjoy, unless they have the financial backing. Despite not having the resources or combined personal experience of these organizations, the Principal may still learn from their methods.

Planning considerations include:

Destination: First, the Principal must find exactly where to go. For most hostile environments it will be a neighboring sovereign that should not extradite the Principal back to the hostile area. The Principal must research the target area first, and then research the neighboring countries to find those likely to support his mission.

The Principal should contact his embassy in those friendly and neutral areas, and ask them about the host nation, its relationship to the target area, the Principal's planned activities, and scheduling and preparation consideration for quickly leaving the target area. Depending on the nature of the operation, the Principal may inquire about the penalties of breaking the customs and border protection laws of the sanctuary nation. Spending some time in a friendly jail is better than spending time at the hands of the Adversary. Note: Embassies do not help in these legal matters, only information gathering, communication, and arranging funds.

Departure: The Principal considers where he will be when he decides to execute the ratline. The start of the ratline should be around the area he conducts most of the clandestine operations. If the Principal plans to work primarily in one area, then his residence and most cover activities should be outside that area to avoid unplanned encounters with Residents. In terms of the ratline, the Principal will discover that he must use it when he is conducting either counter-surveillance for a Resident or during a meeting. If the need to exfiltrate is pressing, but the Adversary is not actively pursuing the Principal, then he may want to start the ratline immediately instead of returning to his cover life. The starting point(s) must have a cache with the necessary supplies to reach the next cache, and should be in areas where he would likely make the decision to leave.

Locals: It is significantly easier to garner support for the cause when the Adversary is oppressing the people. However, if the Principal is working in an area where people are divided on the issue or a majority do not support his goals, then he should not expect much help. Such is the case if the Principal is a Christian missionary in a Sharia region. If this is the case and the locals are very effective with gossip, the Principal may find it difficult to stay hidden.

If leaving the country, the Principal may need help with transportation from people in either the host country or a neighboring country. If the ratline needs this type of support, then the Principal must find it, build strong and loyal relationships with those who can offer it, and eventually recruit them.

Adversary: This is by far the most significant consideration, as this is the ratline's purpose. The Principal must understand how the Adversary controls access to their areas of interest, how they communicate, their search methods, what means of detection they have in areas the Principal passes, and what assets they have and are willing to dedicate to finding him. The route is highly dependent upon this intelligence information. Methods of intelligence collection for this task are elicitation, surveillance, and reconnaissance of the Adversary. At this point of the operation, the Principal does not have an established ratline, so he must keep a very discrete intelligence campaign to avoid detection.

The Principal must know four elements of the Adversary: checkpoints, patrols, observation posts, and reinforcements.

Checkpoints are those access control points that the Adversary mans to scrutinize the public as they move from one area to another. The most common are at border crossings, seaports, and airports. Furthermore, it is also important to know if the Adversary conducts hasty or temporary checkpoints, and how that effects their personnel allocation. The Principal seeks to understand the purposes of these ad hoc checkpoints, if it is to look for people, discover contraband, or extortion. The Principal finds any patterns about when and where the Adversary implements them. If there is a clear pattern on which the Principal can capitalize, he must plan the route accordingly. However, if it proves difficult to see, then he may wish to take more difficult routes to avoid crossing the Adversary.

Patrols and observation posts are two ways of performing the same task of surveillance. The purpose is to see people or things enter and leave their area of interest. There are second order tasks associated with these, which is to either interdict the person or thing, or notify someone who will make the decision to interdict, document, or ignore.

Patrols trade continuous observation for geographic coverage. A patrol's nature is movement, so they can go to areas which observations posts may otherwise be blind. A patrol has a more dynamic perspective, but sacrifices its continuous observation of an area. Conversely, an observation post trades geographic coverage for continuous observation from a desirable vantage point.

An adversary may employ patrols and observation posts together. How many and how effective will differ based on the circumstances of the Adversary. The observation post handles surveillance at a macro level, and the patrols will check blind spots, investigate, and engage any potential threats. When the Principal plans the ratline, he finds observation posts and their blind spots, and tracks the patrols and their routes and schedules. The Principal then finds how these patrols and observation posts might engage him across all environments the Principal intends to cross. This may include: air support, maritime vessels, surveillance-reconnaissance platforms, and so on. This enables the Principal to coordinate his route and timing accordingly.

Reinforcements are the added personnel the Adversary would dedicate to search for the Principal. The Principal should understand how the Adversary would use the added manpower. Some adversaries would send reinforcements to cast a wider net, increase ad hoc checkpoints, increase patrols, or man more observation posts. The Principal must figure out what other manpower the Adversary has, if any, and how quickly they could mobilize them.

As the Principal backward plans, he must name key points where he will stop. Each of these key points marks the beginning or end of a leg. Key points will be caches and safe sites. Reasons for setting up a key point are:

Personal Endurance: Everyone has limits on how far or long he can do something, and the Principal must know his limitations. Therefore, the Principal must take into consideration the frequency and duration of needed rest. Then, the Principal can establish caches and safe sites for when and where he needs them. The healthier the Principal is, the more resilient he becomes, which saves much time and preparation. If the Principal can go 50 miles per day, then the ratline will be much simpler and faster than if he can only travel 10 miles per day. In the planning phase, this is theoretical; when the Principal prepares the route, this may change based on his experiences.

Supply: While the Principal always needs food and water, he may need more supplies for different or successive legs. These may include equipment to get through difficult terrain, like rappelling rope, machetes, and especially communications equipment, like a satellite phone or radio. A benefit of caching is the Principal does not need to haul these supplies with him during travel, making it that much easier. Given, the Principal trades one type of convenience for another, in that added routine maintenance for additional caches is inconvenient.

Environmental changes are transition points. The ratline may take the principal through multiple environments. Therefore, he must have the supplies and equipment needed to handle those environments. If the Principal transitions from urban to rural, then he needs clothes to blend. If transitioning from land to air, then he needs an airstrip or a clearing for the pilot to land and take off. If transitioning from land to sea, the Principal needs swimming equipment, a surfboard, or a kayak, and a place from which to launch.

Scheduling: This is important for coordinating movement like avoiding adversarial patrols or locals, or contacting support Residents for ferrying by air, sea, or land. Safe sites satisfy scheduling, where the Principal can spend as much time as needed without the chances of encountering hostiles. In the urban environment, recruitment may be necessary to elicit aid from a safehouse keeper. A rural safe site follows the same principles outlined in selecting a location for meetings or caches.

Preparing of a ratline includes:

Route Validation: Preparing the legs of a ratline starts when the Principal personally cases the leg. The Principal should travel the leg before use. This gives him an opportunity to take note of difficult terrain and vegetation, how much water and food he may need, what obstacles to overcome, and needed equipment. As the Principal compiles this information, he starts completing and solidifying the route, and gathers needed supplies and equipment.

When casing, the Principal views the activities of both the Adversary and non-hostile persons. It is better to understand their actions, behaviors, and routines when the Principal is not executing the ratline than making a simple, capture-causing mistake. This allows the Principal to avoid problem areas and unintentional encounters with potential threats.

The Principal has at least one alternative route for each leg. Circumstance have a funny way of changing during chaos, and the Principal should have a backup if the primary leg is unsuitable. This is not like a contact where he validates the routes and locations a week or two before use; when a ratline is needed, the Principal may not have many options.

The locations chosen for stops and caches need to be in areas occasionally accessible for validation and maintenance, especially caches. The Principal should not put them so far away it becomes infeasible to emplace and support. Routes tend to either parallel or shortcut more frequented roads or paths. The more capable the Principal, the further his route can be from frequented areas, which lends security.

Caching: Once the Principal knows exactly what he needs for each leg, he then gets those items and caches them. The Principal needs a source of water. If the cache is near a creek or river, then water itself may not need storing, only a filter or purification tablets (iodine). Regardless of the part of the world the Principal is working, these items should be available.

If the ratline will take longer than 24 hours, the Principal needs some sort of food, especially if major legs are by foot. Reserves deplete quickly when activity and stress increases. Whatever the Principal decide to store, he must keep track of any expiry dates and replace them so.

The Principal must execute the various legs of the ratline, but not at once, and take note of what he needs to succeed. The Principal attempts to source the supplies and equipment needed within the area, avoiding adversarial encounters, and caches the contents per the caching chapter.

The Principal must cooperate with and heed the advice of those Residents who aid in the ratline. Residents have skills or equipment the Principal needs, but does not have. If the Principal is going to trust the Resident to help in a very dangerous situation, then the Principal needs to trust the Resident enough to take part in planning. The Principal does not go over the entire route with the Resident, only the sections in which the Resident is involved.

The Principal must never shut the Resident out of a decision. All vehicles have limitations when it comes to natural obstacles. Land vehicles have an easier time, because they use man-made improvements. Marine and aerial vehicles may not have such luxuries during a ratline, so the pickup location will depend on the mariner's or pilot's experience and ability with their craft. If the Resident feels a course of action is a bad idea, the Principal must understand why. If the Resident needs convincing, the Principal must encourage him to discuss his concerns. In the end, they must reach an agreement sincerely. The Principal should never leave an issue unaddressed, lest it worry the Resident and make him less reliable.

The next sections will go into the benefits, limitations, and considerations for each of the four environments.

Urban environments are straight forward. The Principal should spend enough time in the target area to know which locations to pursue, which to avoid, the best ways to get there, and any available alternate routes. Urban environments offer the quickest way of travel on land, because of improved roads. The Principal should try to capitalize on its ease of navigation and speed as much as possible.

Conversely, the Principal is more likely to run into the Adversary or hostile locals in urban environments; this is where most people live. To counter this, the Principal transitions to a different environment, like temporarily traveling though the rural. Sometimes an entire ratline passes through the urban, sometimes a ratline never passes through the urban. Most of the time, legs will go through the urban, like highways on the way to the destination.

Urban considerations include:

Pickups and drop-offs: The Principal should recruit a Resident to drive as much as possible to get to the destination, which maximizes speed and security. When it comes to the Resident picking up the Principal and dropping him off, the Principal should follow many of the methods outlined in the vehicular chapter, with the understanding that the Resident is driving the vehicle. The Principal should still conduct counter-surveillance and only approach the Resident's vehicle when there are no signs of surveillance or threats.

The Principal selects significantly more secluded areas, which have less public traffic; however, it cannot be so far out of the Resident's natural patterns that potential surveillance would consider it suspicious. The Principal considers scheduling for a time when there is no human presence or when others would not consider a pickup suspicious. Furthermore, the Principal selects a location with a secluded foot routes into and out of the site, because he is not in a vehicle upon arrival. The Principal avoids areas with people who may notify the Adversary of his presence.

Counter-surveillance can either be the Principal teaching the Resident surveillance detection routes or offering counter-surveillance support to the Resident. The former is self-explanatory. For the latter, the Principal sets up one or more posts to watch the Resident entering an area, and assesses for surveillance. If no surveillance is present, then the Resident's route should be such that the Principal can get from the observation post to the pickup in time. If the Principal or Resident spots surveillance, then they should have an alternate schedule to retry the pickup at a logical time after the first attempt. If the alternate pickup fails, then the Principal should have an alternate route to get him further along the ratline by foot, which may involve more caches, until he reaches the next obstacle.

Safe sites are places used for timing and rest. When traveling through the urban environment, this is lodging. The Principal should not be renting the room himself, but have a Resident reserve a room for him. The inn must have ways into and out of the room without the front desk or any cameras seeing the Principal. This avoids any potential testimony or evidence that the Resident helped the Principal. If the driver is going to rent the room, the Resident should drop the Principal off out of sight, so no one sees him with the driver. If the Principal use someone else, and prepares this in advance, then he uses a drop to pass the key from this second Resident to the Principal, and back again after he used the room.

Routes the Principal takes are self-explanatory. The Principal maximizes efficiency by using roads, but he should not come across the Adversary. He travels along the road when possible and then moves into the rural to bypass checkpoints or patrols. It may be proper to use the same driver after the check point or patrol later along the leg if there is a suitable cover for the driver to be in the area. Otherwise, the driver went as far as he could and his services are no longer needed.

Caches for the urban include what the Principal needs to complete the leg; however, the nature of human presence may demand that he has some tools if the primary legs fail. A few useful items to consider: lock picks, spring-loaded center punch, adhesive tape, multi-tool, flat-head screwdriver with a non-conductive handle, abundance of local currency, and a change of clothes. If the Principal sets up any signals with Residents, he should keep a suitable signal in the cache in the event he does not bring one with him.

Covers are worthless if the Principal is still in the enemy controlled area. The only place that a cover would matter is at a border crossing. The Principal should not travel through official checkpoints with Residents, even if they are not enemy controlled. It is best if the Principal separates from a Resident before official encounters, including any hasty checkpoints the Principal may come across. However, if the Principal finds himself in a situation needing a cover, then a chance encounter, like if he were hitch-hiking and the Resident picked him up out of the kindness of his heart.

The Principal considers how he communicates with the Resident. If using SMS or cellphones, the phone the Principal uses must be only for this purpose. After they make contact, the Resident removes the record from his phone and the Principal destroys his phone. If asked about it later, then it is a one-off occurrence and the Resident can easily explain away the contact with a wrong number.

In most rural environments, the chances of encountering hostiles are low. The seclusion of the rural offers more flexibility in the Principal's schedules, routes, and safe sites. The Principal primarily uses the rural to bypass enemy encounters, but it can also cut the distances of the routes if there is not enough infrastructure between stops.

Rural environments hinder movement, are more difficult to navigate, and need more planning and preparation to ensure passage. The Principal should minimize his time in the rural. The Principal only spends as much time in it to avoid the Adversary. If the Principal is alone, he is more susceptible to dangers.

Rural considerations include:

Obstacles include terrain, vegetation, and wildlife. Most of the time, the Principal just avoids those areas known to have such obstacles by planning a circumnavigating route. If going around is not possible, because it leads to a hostile area, takes too long, or affords the Adversary an advantage, then the Principal may directly approach the obstacle.

It is much easier to descend difficult terrain than ascend. Rock climbing is not only dangerous, but has two significant vulnerabilities: slow movement up and exposure to anyone in a large area. Conversely, rappelling offers quick descent in a matter of minutes or seconds. If it comes to ascending, the Principal should find a suitable, concealed path up.

Vegetation can be very difficult to pass, especially in the tropics. Often, cutting brush away will slow the Principal down more than a group of people tracking him. In fact, if they get on his trail, the Principal is working harder to clear a path for them as well. The more work he does, the less work they do, so the Principal should avoid these areas. However, if the Principal must clear something, then machetes are useful tools to cache.

Wildlife is not just those beasts that attack humans, but also the small bugs that give people diseases. It does not take much time for diseases to incapacitate the Principal. For larger game, a weapon used to kill them would be well worth mastering and caching. For those bugs carrying diseases, the Principal should allow a protective crust of dirt, sweat, and body hair to develop over his skin, or use certain oils to repel bugs.

Unexploded ordinance often plagues poor or oppressive areas. War torn regions leave these munitions scatter around. The Principal must be very careful to select legs that do not cross areas with such ordinance. This may be tricky, because many of the places the Adversary may wish to defend with landmines also happen to be areas that the Principal must pass to avoid coming across them. If traveling to these types of regions, the embassy should have this information.

Safe sites in the rural are anywhere there is no traffic. The further from civilization, the less risk of compromise. However, there are a few places the Principal should consider more desirable than the open: caves and man-made structures.

Caves offer some of the best shelter and concealment, but it is also a place wildlife frequents. If wildlife is known to be there, the Principal should reconsider using it, especially in inclement weather, where wildlife is more likely to seek shelter.

Man-made structures are nice, but they pose a risk. These are only suitable when neighbors cannot see or hear a squatter's presence. If possible, the Principal may recruit Residents to offer their homes, sheds, or buildings as shelter. These Resident can often aid the Principal in other ways too, with information of adversarial activity or resupply. However, if the Principal cannot recruit someone, he must ensure that he can get in, use the shelter, and leave without the owners knowing. This involves routes and schedules of when to ingress and egress the site.

Caching is more important in the rural when the Principal must travel any significant distance by foot. The Principal works harder and longer in the rural than any other environment. He should plan the caches based on how far he can go and what he would need at the end of the legs. Some of the most basic would be water and food. Depending on where the Principal is and how far he must travel, important supplies include: extra socks, broken-in boots, weapons, animal deterrents, shelters, and candles.

Extra socks are always good and boots are important, because the Principal may not be wearing some at the start of the leg. Animal deterrents include ammonia in a leak-proof bottle, water gun, or soaked rags. Candles offer warmth in small spaces, but should be small enough it does not give away the Principal position.

Routes: The Principal stays at least one terrain feature away from frequented areas, so people will not accidentally stumble upon, see, or hear him. He avoids routes along ridges, so he does not silhouette the skyline. The more or denser the brush he travels through, the more noise he makes, and evidence he leaves behind for trackers. Search parties often travel in groups, which is inherently slower, unless they are in amazing shape and well-coordinated. The Principal takes advantage of this and select his routes to travel faster than a group of people.

Aerial environments are everywhere. It is obvious, but every region on Earth has access to the skies. This is often the quickest way of getting out of an area, as the Principal can travel directly to a destination in a mostly straight line and avoid ground obstacles. The benefit of air travel is even if the Adversary knows the Principal left by air, they will likely neither catch nor attack him. The only way the Adversary can stop the Principal would be deploying personnel to the Principal's destination. Hopefully, that is outside the control of the Adversary.

The vulnerability to exfiltrating by plane is how observable it is. Even if the host government is not involved with the Adversary, flying may attract their attention in a negative way, especially crossing borders. If the Principal stays within all legal constraints, then he should not worry.

Aerial considerations include:

The landing zone is one of the most crucial parts of a pickup. For more information, reference Pathfinder Operations FM 3-21.38. The Principal will still need to learn from his pilot about the aircraft's specific limitations. While helicopters are great vertical take-off and landing vehicles, they are expensive and have their own sets of landing and take-off limitations. Depending on some parts of the world, short take-off and landing vehicles may be the Principal's only choice, which are significantly less expensive, but lack the vertical take-off aspect.

The Principal reconnoiters from the air with the pilot when selecting landing zones. This way both people view the same landscape and are referencing the same observations. If not, the Principal may need to learn as much as he can from the pilot about the requirements, and then select suitable locations by physically casing the areas. Regardless of how the Principal performs reconnaissance, the pilot must confirm and test the landing zone before the Principal executes the ratline. This limits the possibility the pilot would abort the pickup because the Principal did not select a suitable site.

Radar may be a problem for staying undetected by the Adversary. One of the first missions would be to find radar stations, often collocated with airports, but there can be others along the country's border or on naval vessels for defense. To defeat these detection capabilities, pilots use natural, prominent terrain features, which offer coverage from radar, known as naps of the Earth. One of the Principal's tasks is ensuring there would be enough coverage from radar, so the pilot can get in and out without the radar operators seeing it.

Flight paths must afford a safe means for the pilot to take off from his strip, make his way to the pickup and back again without drawing attention. If the pilot stays out of view of radar the entire time, then no one would be the wiser. If there are points where the pilot must drops off radar, then the Principal should seek to understand why that is: out of range of the radar or flying below terrain features.

While terrain features may conceal the pickup from radar, the Principal ensures the ingress and egress routes are also safe from observation. The Principal must first figure out what parts of the flight path needs concealing. Then he figures out if there is suitable terrain that will allow for nap-of-the-Earth flying to get in and out of the area. The Principal must rely on the pilot's knowledge when planning this.

Border crossings can be a significant obstacle. The Principal gets his visas beforehand and avoids crossing borders with much, if any, luggage. Everything the Principal brings into the operational area should be expendable. At this point, the Principal should not give border officials any reason to search or question him. The Principal has the bare minimum, and his only aim now is getting to an international airport to go home.

Covers for the relationship and pickup should not be too far from the truth, because the Principal is now answering to the officials in a friendly or neutral government. The Principal can tell a story about how the pilot saw the Principal stranded or whatever, but the safest course of action is telling the truth: some violent and hostile people pursued the Principal and he called his friend to come get him.

The Principal may suffer a fine or a few nights in jail before the friendly or neutral government lets him go home, but that is much better than the torture or death after extradition back to the hostile area. Host governments' concerns are more with drugs, weapons, other forms of contraband, behaviors that deteriorate their society, or subversion to their authority. They neither want to pay for some naive person's meals nor bear responsibility for his health in their custody. If the Principal poses no threat and makes it very clear he will never return, the authorities may accept a fee or bribe and let him go home.

It is important to note that the Principal should not rely on the assumption that nations who neighbor failed states will aid him fleeing the Adversary. This is something that the Principal must research and confirm. Making a wrong assumption here could be just as atrocious as capture by the Adversary.

Maritime environments are not as ubiquitous as air, but the places that do have suitable waterways can be some of the most secure means of exfiltration. It is much easier to hide in water than air, often because of the terrain features that surround waterways.

The vulnerabilities include adversarial access to boats and their boats' speeds. The boat the Principal finds for support may not be quick and chances are the Adversary will have access to boats that are. It is much easier to commandeer and pilot a boat than a plane; when the Adversary has the same means of transportation as the Principal, there is higher risk.

Maritime considerations include:

The launch point is where the Principal will transition from land to water. This should be around a cache to minimize efforts to haul watercraft to the water. Concealment from any observation posts or patrols is desirable, as well as minimizing exposure in open waters. Once the Principal leaves the shore, he will embark on a friendly vessel, which takes him the rest of the leg.

The embarkation point is the area out from the coast where the Principal boards the boat. The Principal may swim or paddle to the boat instead of boarding the boat at some dock. Due to the limitations of the boat and the terrain underneath the water, the Principal cases with the mariner to ensure that the embarkation point is suitable for both parties.

The embarkation point should be close to or on the mariner's established route, so the pickup does not draw unwanted attention. This also means the Principal must plan the ratline so that it links up with the mariner's route. The embarkation should also limit the duration on the boat with the mariner. If the mariner picks the Principal up deep in enemy controlled territory, then it is easier for the Adversary to get ahead and stop the boat. If the pickup is that much further from where the Adversary starts, then transportation is safer.

Adversarial detection systems include: radar, observation posts, and maritime patrols. These systems are how the Adversary will detect the Principal's exfiltration. The Adversary does not necessarily man radar, but if the government believes the Principal is a hostile actor, authorities may interdict. Interdiction is best in neutral or friendly areas to avoid sending the Principal back to the Adversary. Therefore, the mariner's route should not deviate much to mitigate the appearance of suspicious activities.

The Adversary may very well man observation posts and maritime patrols. The Principal ensures neither the launch point nor the embarkation point are within view of an observation post or maritime patrol. If the Principal must abort this pickup and wait for another pass, then he does so. The Principal does not jeopardize the exfiltration.

Routes need to be as direct and quick as possible, as there is an element of vulnerability when crossing open waters. The Principal minimizes his time on the boat in enemy controlled territory, which also minimizes the mariner's risk.

Caches may have a kayak, raft, surfboard, or similar. Whatever the vessel or device, it should be small and portable. The Principal may schedule a few trips on the boat to case suitable locations for the cache. The first trip to find and assess the locations found on a map with the mariner. The second trip to disembark and case the area on land. The last trip to load the cache with the equipment needed.

Border crossing for maritime exfiltration is like that of crossing the border by air. If the Principal arrives at a port, then he ensures all documents are ready and his visa is current. The Principal may explain the situation and note that he is on his way home. The Principal neither tries to hide in friendly or neutral countries, nor give them a reason to believe he is up to something illicit. He does not spend much time in the sanctuary country. He may visit the embassy or a consulate to get coordination for travel out of the country, but ultimately goes home as soon as possible.

Maritime Law: Oppression usually follows poverty. This should not be that much of an issue, as the Principal tries to travel from one poor and rural land to another. As these boats troll the areas for fish, for example, the goal is to board the boat as close to the coast from which the Principal leaves, and that boat ferries him back to a port that is not in the target area. What the Principal needs to understand is how these nations interact with each other, and what laws apply to these shared waters.

Covers for the relationship with the mariner should be like that of any other Resident. The Principal knew the Resident because the Resident transported the Principal for [enter some cover or pretext]. As for discussing the nature of the ratline leg, the Principal tells the truth: he got into an unpleasant situation and contacted his friend, the mariner; or during a normal route, the mariner saw the Principal paddling out of the area and offered to take the Principal across the border in return for payment. Like the aerial, the Principal may pay a fine or spend a few days in jail before going home. This is much better than capture by the Adversary.

On the environmental permissiveness spectrum, the Principal should only conduct urban meetings in the most permissive environments. Both the general populous and the host nation authorities should either be supportive of or indifferent to the Principal's presence. This will allow the parties to move and meet freely without too much worry someone will notify the Adversary or become hostile.

Public venues are acceptable for assessing a potential Resident, developing a relationship, or seasoning covers. It is acceptable to have other members of the public see the relationship and overhear some of the cover conversations. Although, the Principal must ensure selected venues accept both him and the Resident. Even in permissive environments, personal biases may exist, which the Principal should guard against.

The Principal conducts counter-surveillance support for the Resident in public venues; however, there are mechanics that mitigate the exposure of the contact in such a non-secure location. These contact locations offer some form of temporary concealment from passersby, usually just long enough to pass instructions for the next location. The Principal designs the counter-surveillance route to elicit surveillance behaviors, which allow the Principal to decide whether going ahead with the contact is safe. If the Principal does not detect surveillance, he makes a brief contact with the Principal to set up the primary contact at a semi-secure site. If surveillance is present, then the Principal makes no contact and preserves the Resident's natural patterns.

The purpose of counter-surveillance is to mitigate the risk of the Adversary knowing of the clandestine activities or relationships, which might result in the Adversary forcing their way into the meetings. Often, the Principal has some documents, notes, or equipment that will help the operation's progress, which may also compromise it. If the Adversary suspects the meeting will have such evidence, then they may intrude, leaving the Principal and Resident vulnerable.

When it comes to the semi-secure sites, there must be some form of access control from the public. Restaurants, cafes, bars, lounges, and so on, offer no access control. Anyone can approach, and the Principal has little control over those around him. Hotels, conference rooms, private or VIP sections, and so on, are semi-secure, in that the patrons can expect that no person will stumble into the meeting. This privacy keeps the public from raising concerns about the activities or topics discussed, mitigating adversarial awareness.

The reason these are semi-secure, is because authorities may still enter. Authorities are not just official authorities, but anyone with the will and capability of forcing entry and negatively affecting the operation. The Principal does not need a battle-hardened location for a meeting and often the coordination thereof is not worth it.

The public may see the Principal and Resident enter or leave the meeting site. The Principal must have covers for any potential questions someone raises about the relationship, but no cover for what they discuss or pass in the meeting. In those areas the Adversary is known to intrude, it is important that no compromising equipment, documents, or notes be present; rather, only props that support the cover if the Adversary intrudes.

The Principal avoids establishing safe houses for meetings in less permissive environments, because it introduces many risks: it mixes the Residents' awareness of each other and the Principal avoids using the same locations for multiple meetings, so recruiting a keeper would be quite expensive for a single meeting. The Principal also avoids using abandoned buildings, because there would be no alibi to justify such a meeting. Instead, vehicular or rural meetings would be more proper in more hostile regions.

The Principal avoids clandestine meetings at either his or the Resident's frequented locations, such as home, business, or places of leisure. By meeting at these locations, the Principal has little control over personal interruptions. The cover is there to answer questions, but the Principal should avoid situations that need its deployment. Any interference will need another two weeks planning and preparation to finish what they started. Furthermore, if the Adversary has suspicions, the first places they start surveillance are homes, businesses, and places of leisure. Being that this type of surveillance is likely to have fixed and continuous surveillance, the location may expose the other party to the Adversary.

When conducting an urban contact, the process is: profile, case, validate, and execute. Urban contacts are the easiest to case and more common for normal meeting than any other environment. They are also the most expensive, most vulnerable to casual observation, and the most susceptible to intrusion.

The first step in figuring out suitable sites for contact is developing a site profile. This profile should take into consideration the demographics and characteristics of both parties, the relationship they have together, and what the Principal must do at the location. The Principal has more flexibility than the Resident, but his cover life, demographics, and natural patters are still limiting. The Resident will have similar limits, but with more restriction. Often, the Resident does not have a malleable cover, and he must answer to family, friends, and employers more so than the Principal. This may inherently limit contacts to lunch breaks, a few hours before or after work, and leisure days.

The activity the Principal expects to perform at the meeting location will have the most significant impact on the site choice. Types of activities include: non-sensitive, brief contacts, and operational.

Non-sensitive activities are those that will not lead to compromise if intruded or eavesdropped. If someone were to sit next to the meeting to listen and watch, then they should not glean anything except evidence that supports the cover. The Principal should neither worry nor panic if someone pays more attention than he should; rather, the Principal keeps this eavesdropper in the back of his mind to assess later.

In the paradigm of exposure and logic, these non-sensitive contacts rely significantly more on logic than minimizing exposure. This not as risky, because the Principal sanitizes the contact and there is neither evidence nor discussion of clandestine activities.

Despite not performing sensitive activities at non-sensitive meetings, the Principal still incorporates counter-surveillance before the contact. Depending on the phase of the relationship, the Principal may not teach the Resident counter-surveillance. Doing so may worry the Resident and result in lost rapport. However, when casing, the Principal should seek those establishments where it offers some natural counter-surveillance elements to watch the Resident upon arrival and spot any potential surveillance following him.

Most of the non-sensitive activities will be some public venue. The Principal sets up these meetings to build rapport, further assess the Resident, and solidify the covers. Most relationship rarely start with private meetings. The beginning stages of a relationship are often at public, mutually enjoyed venues. Movies, restaurants, bars, parties, clubs, meetups, fairs, and markets are common venues people attend as their relationship develops. The Principal takes this into consideration and selects venues proper for that phase of the relationship.

The site and its theme must fit within the covers the Principal establishes with the Resident. The Principal selects neither a location where either party would feel uncomfortable nor the other patrons would feel uncomfortable with either party's presence. There are many societies in the world that are sensitive to foreigners, or people of different races, classes, religions, and cultures meeting together. Some societies may even misconstrue two genders as inappropriate. A suitable location would not only allow the either party's demographics, but their presence together does not attract attention.

The Principal should hold urban meetings in neutral or friendly regions whenever possible. Many intelligence agencies specifically look for Residents who have natural, international business or personal travel patterns to such regions. If not, the Principal seeks Residents who have a natural pattern to a neighboring city, preferably one with an abundance of both demographics. This offers much more anonymity and many popular hotels allow for both a foreign Principal and local Resident to enter and exit freely without drawing too much attention.

When the Principal cases a location, he visits it at the days and times he expects to use it. There is little reason for going to a restaurant to decide its suitability in the morning when the meeting will take place in the evening. The day of the week, the time of the day, and any societal celebrations play a significant role in assessing the cross-section of customers at any given location and time. A bar and grill will have quite the different feel and clientele at noon on a Tuesday than at 8:00pm on a Friday. Also, the Principal considers societal events, such as celebrations and sporting events. If there is a national holiday or game playing, people may go out to celebrate, which could alter the suitability of a location.

Conversational topics can be spontaneous. In the clandestine world, spontaneity can be dangerous, especially considering what clandestine relationships are based on. The Resident may bring up something urgent or interesting even though the Principal did not plan for it. Therefore, every location should offer some seclusion, where the meeting can broach such topics quickly; otherwise, it would be wise for the Principal to have a backup location to discuss such sensitivities. Furthermore, seclusion within a venue helps minimize the distraction of constantly assessing those next to the meeting.

The Principal should easily see and assess those entering the meeting location. He should be far enough away to react to any threats without appearing obvious. If the Principal is too close to the entrance when the Adversary arrives, then the Principal's immediate departure may draw attention. Contrast this with being far enough away, the Principal can assess the Adversary's behaviors, leave enough money to satisfy any debts, and excuse himself well before the Adversary could spot him.

This leads into the escape route. The Principal selects a pinpoint location closer to an exit than any entrances a potential threat may appear. The Principal does not necessarily sit next to the exit, which may draw the Adversary's attention at first when looking for a clandestine meeting. When deciding a suitable distance, the Principal takes the following actions into consideration: When a potential threat interrupts a meeting, the Principal expresses that either him or the Resident must leave at once, and depending on the type of establishment, satisfies the check. When leaving, the Principal avoids any threats, and at a pace that is casual, yet purposeful.

Site characteristics that warrant note include:

Payment methods: Cash is king, as it is the quickest to satisfy debts, and once laid on the table, there is no need to wait for someone to run a card, sign, and most importantly try to figure out what to do if the crediting system is down. It is also important to know how much money the Principal needs in preparation to satisfy any debts.

Hours of operation: The Principal notes what days and times the establishment is open. He does not waste time trying to use an establishment that is not open during his planned meeting. It is also important to know peak hours, to avoid customer rushes that may hinder seclusion or prevent use.

Seclusion is how difficult it is to see or eavesdrop on other patrons at a venue. Many venues will have areas that differ in levels of seclusion, sometimes seclusion is uniform. It is important to note these levels during the days and times which the Principal expects to use the site. The Principal quantifies how far others can see or hear, what visual obstructions there are, and how much ambient noise exists to mask a conversation. These metrics will lead to a definitive radius around the proposed meeting spot. If there are areas that are more secluded than others, he names those areas and describe how they are more secluded.

Seat selection: Some establishments assign seating and others allow patrons to choose their own. Regardless, the Principal should know what is acceptable and normal. Even if the establishment allows for patrons to select their seats, but treats the request as odd, the Principal should avoid asking. If the establishment considers requests for seclusion acceptable and accommodates, then it may be a suitable location.

Demographics: The Principal must note what the normal and occasional demographics of a venue are. When the majority of clientele are of one demographic that is different from the intended meeting participants, it does not mean it is unsuitable. Several casings should confidently show whether the location would be acceptable for the Principal and Resident. Characteristics the Principal should take note while casing includes: various ethnicity, attires, payment methods, menu, average and acceptable length of stays, diversity among and between parties, discussions, and attention paid to those outside a party.

Layout: The Principal notes the entrances, exits, restrooms, staff areas, windows, and their opacity, tables and seating arrangements, visual obstacles between areas, and the density of persons in the various sections. Understanding these elements will help plan a proper exit, and assess the seclusion from inside and outside the site.

Service: The Principal notes how helpful or inquisitive the staff are. Sometimes asking many or personal questions is based on the staff member, but other times this is establishment policy. The Principal notes how quick servers return to the table to refill drinks or clear dishes, how often they ask questions, and the nature of those questions. Some discuss only issues relating to service, while others inquire more personally to get to know the customers.

The Principal uses counter-surveillance sites before making clandestine contact. This is optional. It depends on whether the Resident conducts his own surveillance detection and whether the Principal trusts the Resident's assessment. This is rare. Having counter-surveillance support is significantly more reliable, quicker, and more effective than conducting these activities without it. Surveillance detection may take several hours, where proper counter-surveillance support can take minutes. If time is of the essence, it is advisable the Principal offers this support to the Resident.

If the Principal uses counter-surveillance stops, then the Resident should be witting. The Resident must not question why the he is behaving a certain way or executing these activities. This also means that the Principal should brief the Resident on what to do before he does it. The Principal sets aside time during a meeting to give these specific instructions for the Resident to carry out the next contact. Another choice is setting up some impersonal form of communication where the Principal passes these instructions in a secure message, like a dead drop or technical contact.

A characteristic of a suitable counter-surveillance site is a large area. The Principal selects sites with enough space and visual obstacles that any potential surveillance element could not cover the entire area. Surveillance should park and react to the Resident. Examples of these locations include shopping malls, strip malls, bazaars, open markets, stadiums, coliseums, large museums, prominent and populated parks or attractions, and commercial zones. It should include a few locations to set up observation posts to watch surveillance as they react to the Resident's movement and behavior without the Principal needing to move from his observation posts.

Within this large area, the Principal selects a contact point where the Resident waits for the Principal to approach after executing the counter-surveillance route. The Resident should wait at this location for no more than a few minutes. If the Principal finds potential surveillance, a waiting Resident may be an indicator that the Adversary's suspicions are correct. Normal behaviors of others who frequent that location define what a suitable wait time is. The Resident must not wait 30 minutes to make contact when other people in the area are waiting at most five minutes. Likewise, the Resident should not leave after 30 seconds, when everyone else stays a minimum of 20 minutes. The 80% rule applies: the behaviors of the Principal and Resident should fall within the middle 80% of the behaviors of everyone else.

SIDE NOTE: Most of the time, the cover for these meetings are often chance encounters. Something like the Principal happened to see his friend and went over to talk to him. Some may feel the more the Principal uses this cover, the flimsier it becomes. However, the Principal assess inquiries about the relationship and the circumstances of the inquiry. If anyone asks about a relationship's nature more than once, the Principal must assess the security of the operation immediately. It may be that either the selected locations are not suitable, or that the operation is in jeopardy and the Principal must end it.

Lastly, if the parties met several times and later the Adversary interrogates them about these meetings and circumstances, then the Principal has failed surveillance detection, which has little to do with the cover. Not only has the Adversary successfully seen meetings, but the Principal did not protect against it. In conclusion, it is acceptable to use chance encounters as a contextual cover story, knowing that if questioned about it once, it would pass muster. However, the Principal would then assess the Resident and the operation in general. The Principal may have to abandon the operation before the situation becomes worse.

Determining suitability of the initial contact point needs to have some seclusion from other casual passersby. This is significantly more about obstructions to both observation and eavesdropping. When deciding a specific location, the Principal needs obstruction from all directions. If there is much opportunity for others to see or hear the brief conversation, then it is not suitable. The Principal does this by walking the area first as a casual passerby, and then again as the Principal or Resident. The Principal takes note of other's behaviors and the radius of observability, like he did in the restaurant example.

Due to the nature of this location, it is going to be accessible to the public, and it is just a matter of time before another person will stumble into proximity of the meeting. The Principal selects such an unfrequented spot that he can have a complete albeit quick conversation to pass the next meeting instructions before another person might stumble onto this encounter. The Principal spends no more than a few minutes with this conversation, keeping in mind the quicker he passes instructions, the safer the contact. The Principal often rehearses this conversation to get the flow and volume of information passed as efficiently as possible.

The most significant concern is whether someone can listen to the conversation. The topic at this location is going to be very focused and have an air of specific intent. This will not sound like a casual chance encounter between two friends who happen to bump into each other. The Principal passes specific instructions and therefore it will sound exactly like that. The Principal would be wise to include what cover to use in the instructions to aid the Resident if someone questions him about where he is going next.

The Principal should name an alternate location in case someone is occupying the primary location or it is otherwise unusable. The Principal schedules the alternate contact no more than a couple of days from the primary contact, preferably within 24 hours. If people occupy both primary and alternate locations, then the Principal has either not properly assessed the suitability of the site or some inexplicable circumstance arose. The Principal should cancel this meeting and try again at a future time.

While the logic behind the meeting may be flimsy, the cover or the natural patterns, which the Resident relies upon, should not. It is crucial that the general area and the specific point within it fits so well with the Resident that if he is under surveillance, then they will not recognize it is a planned meeting. If the meeting is at a specific store, then it should be one that the Resident would frequent or need.

The Principal must not send a Resident into the business card section of an office supply store if he has no intent on starting a business. Furthermore, the Principal should not instruct the Resident to say such an arbitrary cover. If the Principal desires the Resident to go to a business card section, then the Resident would need a catalyst to want to start a business and then follow the logical steps for someone who is considering such a venture. The Resident would need to research, express this idea to, and accept advice from the people he trusts. Then, after he reaches a point where he needs business cards, would he go buy some. This is important, because lackadaisical covers are exactly the flaws surveillance looks for and if there are inconsistencies in cover and personal circumstance, the Adversary will know that the Resident is working with the Principal who does not do his job well.

The Resident should do what it appears he is doing after the contact. If he goes in to buy something, especially if it is inexpensive or needed, then he should make the purchase; otherwise, it may be obvious that he just went there to briefly meet someone. The Principal should consider giving the Resident money for the purchase beforehand or reimbursing him for the purchases after as a sign of good will, so as not to become a burden on the Resident.

Quantifiable characteristics of this initial contact point include:

Population: The Principal should research the demographics of the population in the area. This location should afford a sense of normality for both Principal and Resident. The Principal neither selects an area that is of one ethnicity, class, or gender, which conflicts with either parties, nor one that would be odd for both parties to meet.

Obstacles: The Principal quantifies the objects and characteristics of the site that offer obstruction to others in the area. If the Principal cases an aisle, he notes the shelves or walls that seclude this point from the rest of the populated area, and how well they give obstruction from that specific spot.

Traffic: If at any moment the Principal sees or hears someone from a direction who is acting normally, there is no obstruction from that direction. If there are intermittent periods of seclusion, the Principal notes how long these periods are. The Principal may loiter without being obvious to note these characteristics. If there is frequent traffic in an area, because it is popular, then the Principal should reconsider using it. The traffic should be infrequent, yet predictable and the time between passersby should be long enough to pass instructions. This will help mitigate accidental discovery of the brief meeting.

Lure: The Principal must name what it is about the spot that draws the Principal and the Resident to it in the sense of a cover story. The Principal notes what purpose it would serve for the Resident to spend time there. This ties back to the natural patterns or motivations for which the Resident is known. This cover must be logical, well known, or easily understandable by potential surveillance.

Time: The Principal notes what an acceptable amount of time is for that specific point. If it is a matter of deciding a purchase, the Principal notes how long the average patron spends deciding such a purchase. It may take several minutes researching the various specs on larger purchases, but it should not take long to decide what type of copy paper the Resident will buy. Similarly, if the Resident is loitering behind a building, it could be the amount of time it takes to smoke a cigarette if the Resident smokes.

Cameras: While the Principal should avoid cameras during non-sensitive meetings, they do not pose as much of a risk in those circumstances as clandestine ones. However, once the nature of the relationship changes where the participants are executing clandestine activities, cameras now make a site unsuitable. At this point, any surveillance would target the Resident. It is one thing to have witness testimony or even a sketch artist (an extreme example), but that is still not as reliable as photographic or audio proof the two parties met. Furthermore, the cover would be easier to defend if there was not such evidence.

The semi-secure location is where the Principal holds a sensitive meeting. The requirements for this type of site are: access control from the public, defensible with covers, at least some level on anonymity, and conducive to bring whatever needed equipment for that meeting.

Access control means that the Principal solely decides who can enter the room or area of the meeting. This usually means there are walls and doors, and those doors have locks the Principal controls. Some VIP sections may offer some seclusion, but if servers or hosts still frequent the area, then it may not be suitable. It is suitable for managers and owners to keep a form of access for pressing or emergency circumstances.

Regardless of access control, the Principal should still behave like any other normal person doing whatever aligns with the cover. If someone knocks at the locked door, the Principal answers. The Principal has a system in place to briefly conceal the tangibles and a procedure in place to change discussion topics and behaviors. The Principal avoids attracting the attention of others, and if he does, he tries to stay in their short-term memory.

The Principal must only select locations the cover supports. The Principal supports the appearance of whatever he is trying to portray. Beneficially, meetings for pleasure and business are common, so many prominent establishments accommodate. Hotels are not just for sleeping, as many business-focused hotels offer rooms for rent by the hour for private meetings or small conferences. Again, this needs booking and payment. The Principal considers dates and times of popular events or seasons, as the cost to rent may increase due to higher demand.

Anonymity is more about hiding in plain sight than trying to prevent any records. If an investigator starts looking and finds data from a hotel, the Principal has a cover. It is more desirable if the hotel accepts methods of anonymous payment, but it is not prohibitive if they do not. A part of casing is to name these types of locations. Even though the world is transitioning more to electronic payment, many parts of the world still use cash. The reason many lodgings prefer credit cards is because they can charge more for damages sustained during the stay and it is much easier for bookkeeping. The organization may waive this if the Principal rents a meeting room for an hour and present himself in a professional and respectable manner.

These semi-secure meetings are to further the operation. Whether bringing maps, computers, special equipment, or supplies, the Principal must have the ability to bring whatever he needs to the meeting without scrutiny. The Principal tests this by bringing comparable items while casing. For example, if the Principal needs a hard-shell container for transportation, then he brings one full of props, which both support his cover and is logical to transport in such a container. Then, if someone enters the room to look around or shows interest in what the Principal is doing, regardless of their pretext, the Principal should find another location.

The Principal performs validation to ensure the assessment of a site is still correct. If the operation will last for a great duration, then the Principal may case sites that he will not use for some time. The Principal uses validation when he chooses a site from a site bank that was cased a while ago. He makes sure it is still suitable. Businesses come and go, change their hours, change their theme or clientele, renovate, and so on. An establishment that once left their customers alone may change their policy to offer more service during private meetings.

Validation is just re-casing the location. The Principal goes through the same steps again with testing reactions to his possessions, watching the behaviors of staff and patrons, confirming payment options, noting observability and eavesdrop-ability, and so on. The Principal must be sensitive to changes and does not hesitate to think a previously suitable site as unsuitable. While this does create more work, it may be the difference between success and failure.

The Principal tries to do everything with the least number of trips possible. He does not want to become a "regular", and thus identifiable upon arrival for the clandestine contact. However, the Principal considers every avenue, which includes understanding the perspectives of potential surveillance, casual passersby, the Principal, and the Resident. Assessing these activities and routes all at once might be too much for a normal person. If it is, then the Principal breaks casing into manageable parts. Validation does not need to be as in depth as the first casing; rather, the Principal just ensures the same features that made the site suitable have not changed.

Execution is following the plans and routes named, while taking into consideration the strengths and vulnerabilities found in casing. During the casing, the Principal finds other avenues for the contact. If there are only three acceptable transition points, three foot-routes from the transition point to the contact point, and only one suitable contact point, then the Principal does not deviate from those. If at the time of execution, something happened to the contact point and the Principal has not found a suitable alternate, then he aborts the meeting and the parties move on to a backup. Accepting uncased locations or unverified behaviors is accepting any failure associated with it.

The key points to take away from this chapter are: understanding when using an urban location is proper (permissive environments), strong covers and normal behavior is of higher importance in this environment than concealment, and these venues, albeit more common and normal in terms of a relationship, are more expensive and vulnerable to investigation.

Rural contacts are the most secure for both parties, and is why the Principal can use it throughout the permissive spectrum. It should be the only choice for the most non-permissive environments, because it may be difficult to set up a car pickup or obtain some semi-secure urban site without drawing unwanted attention. The primary reason for this security is the lack of human presence. Being there is no one to see the contact or the actions leading up to the contact, then there is little threat to the relationship or operation.

The primary circumstances for meeting in the rural are: poverty-stricken regions and outdoorsy Residents, either by occupation, residence, or hobby. Keep in mind that violent extremist group or oppressive regimes often plague poverty-stricken areas, so status covers must be enough to keep the Principal safe when seen in public.

The locations and behaviors need to fit well within the Principal's and Resident's natural patterns. The Principal must not meet in rural environments unless both parties have proven a norm for being there. Most natural patterns should involve travel into or between semi-rural communities, or some occupation or hobby that brings them into the rural environment on a consistent, predictable, or frequent basis.

In terms of cover, both parties should have a well-established natural pattern for being in the rural separately, to the point it needs no explanation to those who know them. Friends, family, and associates should easily corroborate these covers as something for which the parties are known. This is important if the Principal and Resident do not make contact then there is a natural cover for their separate presence.

Furthermore, in the event they make contact, they need an action cover for why the two met in that area and at that time. This does not necessarily have to be as resilient as the natural pattern for being out there separately, but it should satisfy more questions than it raises. Often this will be either a mutual interest in something or a chance encounter.

If the Resident frequents a route, then the Principal should expect others to frequent it too. The predictability of traffic characterizes a route's frequency, not necessarily the volume of traffic. It only takes one person to ruin an operation. If there are not enough regular, predictable gaps between the travelers on a route, then it is not suitable for making contact. If the Principal cannot perform surveillance detection, then he assumes any others in the vicinity are surveillance. The Resident must not leave the trail or road in the presence of another out of concern the other person may be surveillance or may notify the Adversary.

The first step in casing is knowing the Adversary or other parties who would affect the operation. The Principal avoids areas of known adversarial presence or conflicts. The Principal avoids inadvertently stumbling upon an observation post and situations where others may mistake him for an enemy during an Adversary's patrol. The Principal knows which sections of the operational area are of importance to the Adversary or any belligerents to a conflict, and avoids meeting in those areas. The Principal chooses places that offer no advantage to either side of a conflict.

After finding the proper areas for meetings, the Principal obtains maps and imagery, like topographical and trail maps. These maps help find potential terrain pockets between or away from known trails. Just because a trail is not on a map, it does not mean it does not exist. The Principal still cases the site to ensure hidden trails or popular areas are not too close.

The Principal uses imagery to show the vegetation and man-made structures. Some topographical maps offer this information, but not all or it may not be in enough detail to decide suitability. Imagery is neither a human assessment nor generalization like maps are, but a two-dimensional copy of the three-dimensional landscape. Vegetation often changes with season, which may significantly alter the suitability of the site. Obtaining imagery of the area is not a prerequisite, but helps in selecting sites more efficiently.

Lastly, the Resident is the final factor in deciding whether a location is suitable. Just because the Resident is an avid hiker, does not mean he can go hiking anywhere unless he goes hiking everywhere. The Resident's natural patterns limit the Principal's choices. The Principal finds where the Resident frequents, creates a proper natural pattern for himself, and then cases the available area for any potential sites. The Principal must not take the Resident out of his established patterns without first expanding them, which include both the Resident's routes and duration of travel.

While the Principal may case at various times to reconnoiter the terrain, vegetation, or man-made structures, any observations of human behavior are only applicable during the seasons, days, and times he plans the contact. Like that of urban environments, patterns of people in the rural can differ at various times of day and throughout different seasons. The Principal avoids observation in an area dominated by less savory people.

There are five types of locations (four required and one optional) around which the rural contacts will revolve: Resident's natural stops, observation posts, contact points, hasty caches (optional), and meeting sites.

Resident's natural stops: When people travel for any significant distance or time on foot, they will stop to rest along their route. These natural stops play a key role in deciding whether the Resident is under surveillance. While the Principal may abort the mission if anyone else is near the Resident at the contact point, it is important to know whether the Resident is under surveillance in general. The behavior of others in response to the Resident's actions, in this case stopping for rest, is indicative of the third party's purpose for being there. If the Resident is under surveillance, the Principal reevaluates the operation.

Observation posts: The purpose of observation posts is to assess for any potential threats at the Resident's natural stops. The Principal watches others who are traveling with the Resident, if any, and assesses reactions to the Resident at his natural stops. The Principal instructs the Resident to communicate whether he feels safe with some specific behavior or displaying some object that is identifiable from the observation post.

This is a proper time to discuss the options presented to surveillance upon the Resident's stops. The surveillance element may set up some hasty observation post, which can be after passing the Resident or after stopping short out of sight. If there are multiple surveillance operatives, they may rotate: where command continues, backup stops with the Resident or sets up a hasty observation post before the stop, and any others stays out of sight further back. Regardless of the actions, the Principal selects observation posts which afford a good vantage point to see these behaviors. If it appears that the Resident has company at each stop, then the parties do not meet.

While it is less likely, surveillance can stalk the Resident by paralleling through the adjacent brush. Depending on the environment, this may hinder surveillance movement and risk attracting the Resident's attention via noise, movement, or animals' reaction. If applicable, the observation post should have a good vantage point of the area to see any potentially stalking operatives.

Two observation posts are the required minimum to detect surveillance: a post watching over the last intersection or natural stop before the contact point, and another post watching over the contact point with an unobstructed view of both directions. If using the minimum, then the Principal aborts the contact if he sees another person traveling with or near the Resident.

Being the occupation of the first observation post has a time limit, the Principal watches the last intersection or stop for either the sum of time it takes to contact the Resident and travel from the contact point to the meeting site, or enough time it takes for the Resident to be out of sight of the last intersection or stop, whichever duration is longer. This ensures a suitable time window to counter any surveillance missed after leaving the first observation post.

The first observation post should have enough over-watch to view both the last intersection or stop, and the point at which the Resident would no longer be visible from that intersection or stop. The contact point's observation post should see far enough in each direction that by the time any passersby cross the contact point, the Principal and the Resident are out of sight and sound. Even though the Principal theoretically cleared the direction from which the Resident is traveling, he must not neglect it, as this is his last line of defense in the event something extraordinary happens.

These observation posts do not have to be off the trails and in the bush. If the Principal can logically and discretely see these important points of the Resident's route from the same or adjacent trail, then he may do so. However, an observation post on the same route will not likely offer much of a vantage point to confidently assess the seclusion of the contact. The exception is the observation post of the contact point, which will be at some point between the contact and the meeting site. The cover should be enough to have a brief encounter on the trail, but offer a polite excuse if anyone else shows up near the contact.

If the Principal has trusted friends or associates, having them occupy the observations posts will exponentially increases the reliability and security of the meeting. This way, the Principal does not have to sacrifice time at some of these location, or make too many movements in the brush, which can be dangerous, noisy, or slow. If support is available, then the Principal needs some form of communication to securely pass information to and from the other counter-surveillance support. This will help prevent any amateur radio or adversarial SIGINT operators from intercepting.

One example would be to devise a system of squelches over a radio. This system should include: the stop or observation post identifier, whether the Resident has company, and whether the Resident is showing the safe signal. Furthermore, the Resident needs a signal to distinguish him from anyone else who may be on the route; this prevents support from mistaking the Resident for someone else, or someone else as the Resident.

Contact point is the point the Principal reaches out to the Resident to bring him to the meeting site, which means this is also the point where the Resident deviates from his natural patterns. This is where the mission crosses over from the normal life to the clandestine one, and as such involves some serious risk.

Primarily, the Principal ensures there is adequate concealment at this point, so no one else can see the contact or the movement to the meeting site. He also ensures there are no other vantage points to this location along adjacent trails, where a casual passerby could inadvertently see the contact or the parties leaving the path. The Principal studies the maps to find ridges and peaks, and reconnoiters for spots that have a clear view of the contact point.

Next, the Principal makes contact. Being that no other travelers are on the path near the Resident, the Principal can securely approach the Resident personally by interdicting him on the trail. However, the Principal may devise an auditory or visual signal to draw the Resident off the trail toward the Principal, making the first contact a few yards from a normal path.

Hasty caches can help if the meetings need compromising materials. The Principal can load the cache upon arrival to the area or on the way to the contact point, and then unload on the way to the meeting after making contact. The purpose of the hasty cache is to relinquish possession of compromising evidence in the event the Principal missed surveillance or a hostile confronts the

Principal. Even if the Adversary finds the cache, there is still deniability, except when the contents of the cache can name either party.

This is a good point to bring up short hand. The Principal should consider developing his own short hand, or learning another language. If someone finds his notes, then it may add a layer of security between potentially compromising evidence and the Principal.

After the meeting, the Principal may wish to reload the cache with the compromising materials while he performs surveillance detection. If the Principal did attract surveillance and they stop and search the Principal, he will not have any compromising materials. The Principal would then make another mission to retrieve the notes and materials as soon as he decides he is clear. This is at the Principal's discretion.

Meeting sites are the secluded locations where the Principal and Resident meet. While true, the further from the populated areas the more secure the site; however, there is a diminishing effect. There is a point where any further from populated areas offers no added security, but continues to use valuable time and resources. The meeting site should be as close to the Resident's natural patterns without sacrificing the characteristics that make it secure.

These meeting sites can take many forms, whether on secluded side trails or roads, natural draws into a secluded area, or locations not accessible through any path, natural or man-made. Regardless of how these sites manifest themselves, the point is the intermediate area secludes and protects the site from sight and sound of more populated routes or areas.

Distance through or over natural features gives seclusion in the rural. These features include vegetation and terrain. During casing, the Principal decides what distance is enough to protect the meeting. The Principal quantifies these levels of protection in the form of a radius. The Principal does this by watching and listening to others in the area from either the perspective of the Principal, Resident, or a casual passerby.

Military units have a technique known as the cloverleaf. When setting up a rendezvous or encampment, the unit will perform a cloverleaf to ensure there are no threats or concerns in the immediate area. The patrol leaves in one cardinal direction and loops back around to an adjacent cardinal direction, and repeats this for all directions.

The Principal ensures there is no other trail, campsite, road, point of interest, or some frequented area next to the meeting site. The Principal looks for more than the obvious signs, like worn paths or man-made clearings, but smaller, more subtle signs. He looks for any types of trash, broken twigs or branches where people would kick or step, carvings on trees, and so on. The Principal avoids locations where children, adolescence, or nefarious groups may use as a secret rendezvous.

The distance traveled for the cloverleaf is at least the same distance set up initially in the seclusion radius. The denser the vegetation or more prominent the terrain, the less distance the site needs for security. Crossing over prominent terrain features may draw attention as the parties might silhouette the skyline. The Principal uses minor terrain features to separate the meeting site from the other frequented routes and areas. Area familiarization eventually leads the Principal to noticing interesting, natural pockets and paths that make good meeting locations. It is a matter of performing due diligence. It helps if the Principal is in good physical condition.

The departure point is like the contact point, but instead of going from the route to the meeting site, this is going from the meeting site back out to the route. The departure point should be different from the contact point. It should be further along the Resident's route, inviting a logical flow. Aside from this, the departure point shares many of the same characteristics as the contact point. The Principal should have an observation post to ensure that no one else is at the departure point when the Resident returns to his route, and it should have enough concealment from each direction on the route and from any other potential vantage points.

The routes to case include: infiltration, observation, meeting, emergency, abort, and exfiltration. This would be a proper time to pick up a book on military land navigation and operations in rural terrain. This other reading includes the principles of navigation through unimproved or desolate areas, movement techniques, and route planning considerations. While the Principal may not have to travel great distances from beaten paths, he could easily lose his bearings if he does not know what to do. It is best to start getting comfortable with land navigation and movement in the wild.

When casing each route, the Principal takes note of:

How long it takes to travel the various legs of the route. This includes how fast the Resident walks, how fast others walk, and how fast the Principal walks.

Any potential threats or obstacles along the route. If obstacles exist, the Principal understands how these obstacles would affect the mission. For example, in the case of searches, the Principal needs to know the purpose of the search, what the searchers are looking for, and where they look. The Principal decides if the potential encounter would be a threat to the operation or just an inconvenience.

The demographics of the route if applicable. If the route or area is of one demographic, then the Principal needs to know the potential of the Adversary scrutinizing, stopping, questioning, or searching him.

The traffic and its clear times. The less traffic during the planned meeting, the more secure it will be. Only those routes that offer seclusion to leave and re-enter the trails or roads during meeting times are suitable.

Anything else the Principal feels would help or hinder movement as it pertains to the purpose of executing the route. The requirements may differ between the distinct types of routes.

Infiltration: Even if the area is permissive, the Resident may still be under surveillance upon his arrival to the contact. The Principal avoids signaling his presence or identity. This usually means that the Principal approaches the area or route from an oblique direction. If the Principal drives to the general area, he parks outside the vicinity of where the Resident parks. The Principal may cut through the brush from an adjacent trail or road to avoid observation on the same route as the Resident.

The infiltration route involves:

Starting point: Where the Principal begins his movement to the area. This is often a staging area after conducting surveillance detection.

Directions to the debarkation point: From a prominent landmark to the last point before leaving a normal road or path. The debarkation point is where the Principal switches from normal to questionable behavior, like trekking off into the brush. This may be a transition point from vehicular to foot travel.

Waypoints to the destination: This is the route from the debarkation point to the destination, which is the first observation post or hasty cache. These can be the most crucial part of the infiltration, as it is the part where most people would lose their way. This is where the Principal implements the skills he obtained from studying and practicing land navigation.

Observation route connects the observation posts. The Principal's plans accommodate the time it takes to move between posts. The Principal must arrive at the next observation post before the Resident gets to his corresponding stop. Each leg between observation posts needs a series of way points to navigate from one to the other. The last leg of this route is from the contact point's observation post to the contact point, which should not be that far and an easy route to execute.

Meeting route: This is the route the Resident takes if everything goes to plan. This includes where he arrives to the area, the paths to his cover stops, the contact point, the meeting site, the return to the cover route, and his exit from the area. The only part of this route that includes the Principal is making contact, traveling to the meeting, and leaving from the contact. This route is about the Resident.

Emergency route: This route is optional, and one the Principal executes to flee the meeting. Whether the Resident goes with the Principal during escape is optional; the Principal decides this on a case by case basis. The purpose is an emergency exfiltration from the area before the Adversary has a chance to engage the Principal. The Principal needs to decide if either or both parties escape. Some circumstances make confronting the Adversary or authorities with a cover more secure than trying to run.

Abort route: This route is also only for the Resident, and is the normal route the Resident takes if the parties do not meet. This means his natural pattern. An exception is if the Principal uses a signal to draw the Resident from the natural path. The abort route would include this new segment to and from.

Exfiltration route: This is the Principal's final route out of the area, after making contact. This is like the infiltration route, except backwards: from the break in contact with the Resident to where the Principal begins surveillance detection again, and all the waypoints in between. From there, the Principal either caches any compromising items or returns to his cover life.

A major concern is being able to find the locations again. It can be very easy to lose his way if the Principal must travel a few hundred meters between points. Maps brought to meetings should not have observation posts, cover stops, contact point, meeting site, infiltration, exfiltration, or emergency routes, or check points. The Principal memorizes these important points, along with using expedient land navigation methods and prominent features to help guide him throughout the area.

Pinpointing these operational locations is like land navigation, except at a micro level. While land navigation uses a series of major and minor terrain features identifiable on a map, the Principal uses the micro features only identifiable through direct observation. He uses nature and its mutations to help guide him to these points. These should be objects and features that are so uncommon that they are obvious. A couple of examples are mutated trees, massive or oddly shaped boulders, rocks, or formations thereof, caves, streams, clearings, grouped vegetation, and so on.

The amount of daisy chaining depends on how easy it is to navigate through the brush. Sometimes the Principal needs three legs to get from one point to another, other times ten. This will completely depend upon the Principal, the environment, and how prominent these locations are.

Lastly, once the Principal finds a site, he details the terrain and vegetation in each cardinal direction; this allows him to verify the exact spot later when he prepares for the actual meeting. The Principal names three prominent features or objects that stand out in different directions from the operational location. This will confirm the location during validation. It is common for people to be off by several meters, and end up at a point vulnerable to casual passersby.

The key points to take away from this chapter are: understanding when using a rural location is proper (least permissive environments), concealment and seclusion are of higher importance than strong covers and normal behavior, and these environments are some of the most secure, as long as the Resident's natural patterns are conducive.

Vehicular contacts offer more security than urban contacts and more flexibility than rural. Except those in the most poverty stricken rural or oppressive regions, the Principal can make vehicular contact most anywhere. The mobility of vehicular contacts lends to their security. The meeting is not in the presence of anyone long enough to recognize either the Principal or Resident, let alone eavesdrop on the conversation. Furthermore, people pay more attention to the vehicle itself instead of the occupants, which offers another degree of concealment.

The vehicular meeting is a way to meet the Resident in the urban when the environment is not the most permissive. This is especially true for regions where the Principal's demographics would generate some gossip if seen and even more so when he is with a local. Contrast this with trying to meet the Resident face-to-face at some hotel or conference room, and the desk finds the Principal's presence discussion-worthy, or the worst case, someone calls the Adversary.

Vehicular meetings can be more logical than other meeting venues when considering the Resident's personal circumstances and natural patterns. Offering him a ride would not be as odd or difficult to explain when the Principal has an established cover with the Resident than trying to explain why they are trekking off the beaten path.

The vehicular can start or end in either the urban or rural environment if the contact follows the principles of security. These principles are very much like the initial contacts made in the urban when passing instructions to the primary meeting. The universal principles of exposure and logic apply. In the less permissive environments, especially those involving more scrutiny, limiting exposure is more important than ensuring logic.

The Principal neglects neither exposure nor logic completely. This means neither trying to pickup or drop-off the Resident in areas that make no sense to his natural patterns nor in the completely open locations for any to see. Often, this will involve a route to an area that will offer some seclusion from the rest of the population.

One of the biggest considerations for vehicular casing is exact timing. The Principal executes most of these with a window of only a few moments where the principles of exposure and logic are suitable. Therefore, when the Principal cases these locations and routes, he ensures the parties' routes intersect at the most opportune time.

The down side to a vehicular contact is the time and cover requirements. This usually means the Resident dedicates a significant part to "errands". The moving parts a vehicular contact can make this difficult to plan or at times prohibitive to use.

The Principal must case six routes for the vehicular: surveillance detection, pickup route, abort route, primary meeting route, alternate meeting route, and drop-off route.

The surveillance detection route includes a series of stops, legs, and observation posts.

Observation posts are where the Principal watches the Resident as he makes cover stops. These posts must have a good command of the area to spot the presence of surveillance. Depending on the circumstances and how permissive the environment, the Principal may perform this from his vehicle to stay hidden. If exiting the vehicle for counter-surveillance support, the Principal coordinates the timing of getting back to the vehicle and then drive to the pickup.

While minimizing movements is best, it will be up to the Principal whether to set up more than one observation post throughout the Resident's surveillance detection route. Potential surveillance will look for anyone supporting the Resident in clandestine activities, so the Principal should minimize his movements to avoid the risk of drawing attention to himself.

If the Principal decides to exit the vehicle to do counter-surveillance support on foot, he should park his vehicle near the end of the route, so he can reach the pickup without going back to the beginning. This is relevant for doing surveillance detection at venues that are more linear at larger distances. How much time it takes the Resident to get from the last cover stop to the pickup, plus the time the Principal takes to retrieve the vehicle and get to the pickup will decide the Principal's parking location. Most of the time, the Principal performs counter-surveillance support inside the vehicle from a single observation post.

Cover stops are the stops that the Resident visits to elicit any surveillance presence. At this point, the Principal performed surveillance detection to ensure that he did not bring surveillance to the contact. As for the Resident, he may not have enough time in his schedule to conduct his own surveillance detection. Regardless, it takes less time if the Principal condenses surveillance detection activities by supporting the Resident than having the Resident do so on his own.

Stops should have some tie to the Resident's natural patterns and personal circumstances. The Resident only visits those establishments which fit his legitimate needs or wants. The importance for assessing the Resident on these factors is so the Principal can ensure he does not violate these patterns. The Principal may expand the Resident's patterns to create more contact choices, but the Principal must do so naturally and smoothly. The Principal avoids abrupt and aggressive changes in the Resident's patterns, minimizing questions from family, friends, or the Adversary.

Stops need to entice the surveillance to go inside with the Resident. If the stop is completely open, and in the view of anyone outside, then any potential surveillance will not go inside. Furthermore, enticement would come from the suitability of using that venue for some type of clandestine activity, such as a brief encounter, brush pass, or dead drop.

The surveillance effort may only send one operative at a time to enter with the Resident, and then rotate operatives as the Resident visits other stops. The Principal keeps track of those who arrive with the Resident and set up observation posts. The Principal watches those vehicles dropping off one or two passengers at the same stop as the Resident and others who park without getting out. If those who parked have only one passenger get out and later enters a successive stop with the Resident, then the Principal should abort the meeting.

Lastly, the stops should be logical in terms of the Resident's current cover activities. The Resident must not frequent the same general stores selling the same products. There may be an element of shopping for a good deal, but that should only be the case if it is a part of the Resident's natural patterns. The Resident must not change his behaviors for operational convenience, when it would in fact pose a threat to security. Again, surveillance is very sensitive to these changes in behavior, so the Principal ensures the Resident is behaving naturally during periods of surveillance uncertainty.

Regarding multiple observations posts, the Principal ensures he can reach his next observation post before the Resident reaches the next stop. The Resident's route may need timing stops to keep the Principal's observation posts synchronous. The Principal cases each leg of the surveillance detection route for both the Principal and Resident, scrutinizing the time for each leg of each party, and adds timing stops appropriately.

Pickup routes have two routes, one for each party. They start from the last point during surveillance detection and end at the pickup. Either party's route may have a timing stop and the routes intersect at the pickup location.

Timing stops: the parties use these stops to synchronize coordination between the Principal's vehicular route and the

Resident's foot route. Depending on which route would be quicker to the pickup, the closer party's route would need to have a location where that party can pause before making the final approach. If it takes the Principal three minutes to travel from the last observation post to the pickup, and the Resident 30 seconds from last cover stop to the pickup, then the Resident needs to stop for two minutes and 30 seconds to synchronize. Conversely, the Principal may wait at his last observation post for an added two minutes and 30 seconds before leaving for the pickup. The timing stop is like any other stop: it needs to adhere to the covers, patterns, and customs to keep from appearing suspicious.

The pickup is the vulnerable point where the normal life transitions to the clandestine one. However, because the parties executed surveillance detection before the pickup, the threat is more likely from casual passersby who may find it odd or discussion worthy that the Resident is getting into a vehicle with the Principal. Therefore, to reduce this risk:

The Principal avoids cameras, especially if it is a less permissive environment, to prevent some form of photographic or video evidence of the Resident entering the Principal's vehicle. If the Adversary or an informant sees the contact, then investigators will canvas the area looking for evidence. If there is footage, then they now have several leads, such as the vehicle used. Cameras watching the proposed pickup make the site unsuitable.

The pickup must be a secluded part of the Resident's route, and his route must be something he would naturally take. If the Resident is known to avoid alleys, it would be suspicious if he suddenly went down one. Proper obstacles should separate the pickup from the more frequented areas or routes of others. Obstacles in this context are features, natural or man-made, which hinder the observation by others. In the urban environments, common obstacles are buildings, walls, fences, decorative shrubs, and so on. In the rural environments, obstacles are terrain features and vegetation. Depending on the vehicle, it can offer an element of concealment for the pickup, granted that it is tall enough and the windows are opaque.

To help illustrate this, each direction needs to offer some element of protection from someone seeing the pickup. First, the Principal considers each direction from that point, and then mentally removes the presence of humans. The Principal notes from that point the nearest obstruction.

The next part of deciding seclusion is to add human presence and activity again. There are two parts to considering human presence: presence at or in the view of the pickup.

If the parties can travel along this route, then others can too. The point of casing is to find the frequency of others on that route. The Principal ensures enough window for both parties to enter this area, make contact, and leave together without someone else on the same route seeing the pickup.

Next, the Principal limits the visibility of the pickup from the more frequented routes and areas. The Principal does this by selecting locations that have most viewing angles obstructed. However, there are clear views to the location, because a vehicle needs to enter and exit the area, and there should be two. Single entrance-exit locations impede the movement and flow and may draw attention from casual bystanders.

There are very few locations that offer complete seclusion from human presence or activity for any significant period. The only examples of complete obstruction in the urban environment would be "U" or "S" shaped allies and parking garages, where walls surround the location in all directions from the most frequented areas. If the Principal finds some, and they fit within the Resident's natural patterns and personal circumstances, he uses them. If not, the Principal minimizes exposure of the pickup from any give person. There are a few ways to do this:

Use "L" or "I" shaped allies, the traffic at the exposed ends should be flowing enough that any one person would not have enough time to see and mentally register the pickup. This also means that the Principal considers aborting if the exposed ends of the ally have any stagnant traffic or loitering persons.

Limit the exposure between points of concealment via flow. Buildings offer visual obstructions between those inside and those outside; this can help the pickup. If the Principal times the routes properly, it would be enough for the Resident to leave a building and immediately get into the vehicle. The Principal ensures the Resident does not do this in the view of the exit as that offers clear sight of the pickup from those inside the building. It is best if the Resident turns and travels just enough to clear the exit before entering the vehicle.

Use a secluded part of a rural road. If the Resident is known to travel on foot along these more desolate roads, then using the natural vegetation and terrain can be enough. The Principal ensures he comes from behind the Resident as a final effort that they are not under surveillance. For more information on conducting counter surveillance in the rural and planning this type of hybrid meeting, reference the rural chapter. The difference is after the last cover stop and observation post, the Principal retrieves the vehicle and make it to the contact point (in this case the pickup) by the time the Resident does.

The pickup location can be a timing stop too, and this would be an example of a fixed pickup. These offer an element of risk as it can appear as loitering, which attracts unwanted attention; however, this can help with timing for suitable location that do not have a good window of opportunity. The Principal ensures a suitable cover activity the Resident performs to alleviate perceived concerns before the pickup. The most common activities are smoking and using a phone.

Lastly, the pickup must be outside of the theoretical surveillance box. Surveillance sets this up around the Resident's last transition point upon entering the area. Having it outside the housing box is one more surveillance elicitation technique and offers more security. By taking the Resident outside the box area, the surveillance team will try to reestablish the box and parallel positions around the Resident as he travels on foot, which is easier to see than stationary surveillance posts. Secondly, by ensuring the pickup is outside the box, it prevents the possibility of fixed surveillance positions watching the pickup.

Abort route is like a cover route, but includes an abort stop. Instructions to the Resident includes how and where to enter the area, the stops he will visit in that area, how and where to travel between stops, cover activities, and durations of visit. The Principal avoids telling the Resident the exact pickup point, just that it will take place along the described route. Eventually, the pickups will become obvious during the briefing, but it is important that the Resident does not predict the Principal's actions, as surveillance may see anticipation in the Resident's behaviors.

The abort stop is a cover stop, but one without an observation post. The purpose of this stop is to give the Resident a logical reason to travel through the pickup. If there is surveillance or an attentive casual bystander, then the Principal aborts the mission and the Resident continues his way to the abort stop before returning to his normal life.

Pickup routes are either linear or circular. Linear paths allow the reuse of a suitable pickup location in the event a fluke incident causes an abort. After a significant period, it may be possible to try the pickup again as the Resident travels back to where he arrived in the area. This will be completely dependent upon the Resident's natural patterns and personal circumstances, like if the first location is where the Resident must return. Circular offers no other advantages, it is a onetime pass before returning to cover lives.

Primary meeting route is the route taken once the parties execute the pickup. There are a few considerations when selecting a route for a meeting:

Schedule: The Resident will only have so many minutes or hours to meet. The Principal cases a route that will accommodate this time constraint. The traffic patterns during the seasons, days, and times of scheduled meetings must be such that the meeting will not interfere with the Resident's natural patterns.

Cover: It is important to understand the potential interrogatives surrounding the contact. As with most contacts, the options are either a planned or a chance encounter.

If this is a planned encounter, initial questions include: Why the Principal picked the Resident up at that location. When and how the parties coordinated this encounter; if by phone, the parties must have corroborating phone records. What the purpose of the encounter is. Where the participants traveled and why that route.

If this is a chance encounter, initial interrogatives include: What each participant was doing in the area and evidence thereof. Why meeting was urgent enough to pursue it right then, but not urgent enough to call or schedule an appointment. Why either or both took the specific route they did.

The last question may associate with the relationship cover or it can be something where the Principal saw the Resident walking and he wanted to give him a ride while they talk about some cover topic. This also means that the Principal took the Resident to that location, which means he must case it, it must fit within the Resident's natural patterns, and if the Resident told people where he was going, then it should be a logical destination.

An example is the Resident expresses to someone that he plans to run errands, which includes going to a few stores. First maybe a market, and then later to a specialty store that is a bit out of the way. Both the Principal and Resident were in the market doing [action cover], the Principal saw the Resident walking toward the [pickup]. The Principal went to see if the Resident had time to discuss [relationship cover]. The Resident was heading to the specialty store, which offered the perfect opportunity to talk in route to the Resident's next errand.

Adversarial or nefarious presence: The Principal avoids threatening checkpoints and patrols, or any other activities that involve searches, scrutiny, or extortion along the meeting route. The Principal finds patterns or regions where most of these take place and avoids them. If these adversarial or nefarious activities are so unpredictable in location and time that they can happen anywhere at any time, the Principal can change the vehicular contact tactics.

Common examples of this include gangs in countries with weak governments or Islamic extremists in the middle east or Africa, where they randomly set up hasty checkpoints. This can be very dangerous especially in possession of notes or materials that would show some form of clandestine activity during the meeting.

To assess the threat level of the operation, the Principal decides how these groups respond to those who avoid checkpoints. He notes whether the hostile group would pursue anyone they saw turning around or detouring.

There are a few ways to help mitigate this, but would need more planning and preparation. First, the Principal considers urban or rural meetings and whether they would be more proper or secure. If not, then to minimize movement, the Principal may hold meetings in secluded areas, so the participants do not inadvertently run into these groups. This is a modified vehicular contact, but instead of moving, the location is static.

When finding a suitable route or point, it needs to adhere to why a vehicular contact is secure: No one person is in proximity long enough to see either party, and no one can eavesdrop on what the parties discuss. If the Principal decides to park, then the traffic needs to be as such that the passersby are moving and not coming back. This can be very difficult to find. If used, a suitable cover needs to answer why they stopped at that location and not at the destination or pickup.

Segregated areas: This relates to being out of place from the norm. If the Principal is in a culturally, ethnically, or class diverse area, then he will not stand out as much from others. However, if there are areas or neighborhoods that are mostly one demographic, then unless the parties fit within that mold the Principal avoids them, especially if they have members who investigate or intimidate outsiders.

Incorporate counter-surveillance techniques: Along the route, the Principal includes elements such as corridors, choke-points, change of venue, and so on. This will help with any unseen surveillance elements before the pickup and allow the Principal to respond properly. The Principal avoids cover stops along the route, because that would involve unnecessary exposure to locals. However, the Principal includes some of the route characteristics mentioned in the counter-surveillance chapter.

Alternate meeting routes may be optional depending on the cover of the meeting. For example, if the Principal sets up a route that addresses a common cover, but the Resident has an abnormal time constraint, then the Principal must cut the meeting short. If the Principal use the cover of giving the Resident a ride to a faraway location, he may be able to conduct a full meeting in the time it takes to drive there. If it is proper, there would not be an alternate route, unless as a contingency for security. However, if the destination is not far and the meeting needs more time, then the Principal has a longer primary and shorter alternate in case of abnormal time constraints.

The Principal cases alternate routes the same as primaries, because their considerations are the same. When it comes to answering the questions of how short should this route be and what if the time constraint is shorter than the already short alternate route, then the Principal considers the least required times to meet. If the Principal needs 30 minutes to discuss all the topics, but the Resident does not have that much time, then the Principal should abort the meeting and the parties try again at the backup.

This is not about what the Principal wants; rather, it is whether there is enough time to satisfy the basic needs, lest reestablish contact. When setting up signals or making initial contact, the Principal ensures the Resident can easily and quickly communicate that he is available for the absolute least time needed. If not, the parties break contact and execute the backup. If so, the meeting starts and the Principal decides the route based on how much time the Resident has.

Once the Principal finds suitable routes for the meeting, he executes the route behaving like the middle 80% of other drivers. He breaks no enforced laws, and behaves just as those who get by without drawing attention.

The drop-off is very much like that of the pickup in that it should have the same level of obstruction, seclusion, and limited exposure. The difference lies in the flow's reversal, so the Resident should exit the vehicle and move into a cover stop without anyone associating him with the vehicle.

Drop-off routes starts with the final approach to the drop-off location together, executing the drop-off, and continuing separately back to respective cover lives. The final approach beings when the Principal makes the first turn from what would be a more frequented route to navigate the drop-off.

The drop-off cannot be within the same area as the pickup; it should be outside of the theoretical surveillance box of the pickup, as well as the theoretical box of where the Resident entered the area. That means two separate theoretical surveillance boxes that the drop-off cannot be within.

If the Principal drops off the Resident near the pickup as a matter of convenience, the drop-off should be in the same direction from the pickup as the abort stop. An example is, if the Resident walked South towards the abort stop, then the drop-off should be South. This way any surveillance would see the Resident coming from that same direction

It may also be proper to have the Resident take a taxi back to the abort stop, which it outside both theoretical boxes, and return along a similar route back to his original transition point. This will depend on the timing and operational circumstances.

Now, much of this may not be applicable if the Resident relies on public transportation and taxis. If that is the case, then the Resident may not need to return to the original transition point, and the Principal may drop him off wherever is most convenient and proper. Again, this is completely dependent upon the Resident's personal circumstances and natural patterns, like whether he has a car and whether he uses it, respectively.

The drop-off route will lead to the first stop of the surveillance detection route to ensure that the Principal did not attract the Adversary or nefarious attention from either the meeting route or the activities at the drop-off. Once the Principal is confident that he is not under surveillance, he returns to his cover life.

The key points to take away from this chapter are: understanding when using a vehicular meeting is proper (semi or moderately permissive environments), concealment and flow have a greater impact than strong covers and normal behavior, and these methods of contact are more secure than urban and more flexible than rural.

Technical contacts are those only achieved through some special equipment. This can be through a phone, computer, facsimile machine, or similar. Technical contact needs both parties to have access the medium through which they make contact. As of now, technical communications involve the manipulation of electromagnetic radiation. Humans cannot modulate and demodulate pulses of radio waves in the air or electronic signals through a wire, so they need some machine to translate between what humans can see and these signals.

The greatest benefit of technical communication is how two people can pass information without being in close physical proximity. A secure communication medium, accessible by both parties, alleviates much of the vulnerability associated with making physical contact. Unfortunately, the telecommunications industry heavily watches these communication mediums. Furthermore, because machines automate tasks, the industry, authorities, or the Adversary may only need a few people to watch these mediums for clandestine activities.

This is particularly troublesome, because the nature of the operational goals often has at least one party in an adversarial controlled region. This means if the Adversary can track the general population, then the Principal or Resident are at risk when openly communicating over networks or radio. This is not the Wild West Web of the 1980s and is not as anonymous as it once was.

As hackers of decades past took advantage of anonymity of the internet, the security industry became more robust to combat those efforts. Thus, much of the world has developed monitoring systems and countermeasures to protect against illicit actors. While the industry developed these technical surveillance methods to catch criminals, the industry also discovered these systems work equally well on user of public networks. This gave birth to cyber spying.

In the beginning, intelligence agencies, militaries, and governments performed technical surveillance against radio transmissions, or signals, mostly associated with WWII. The term for intelligence derived from these intercepts is Signals Intelligence or SIGINT. As technology advanced to protect these signals, so did the technology to break these protections. Sometime these security agencies crack the encryption algorithm, sometimes they crack the keys, and other times they crack the human users. Regardless of the methods used to gather useful information, the world became exceedingly good at gathering intelligence information from telecommunications. Thus, the Principal cannot rely on the technology itself to safeguard communications. Instead, he must deceive the humans building and using the systems.

Communications break down into a matrix, where on one axis is "secure" and "unsecure", and on the other axis is "physical" and "virtual". Secure communications in the context of this chapter are those communications perceived meaningless to the Adversary if intercepted, while unsecure communications are meaningful. Virtual and physical relate to the ability to send and receive communications with or without some technical augmentation. To access the cyber world, humans need some machine to do so, and thus is the requirement to enter the world of virtual communications or telecommunications.

This matrix yields four categories: secure-physical, unsecure-physical, secure-virtual, and unsecure-virtual. To put these into perspective, the other chapters discuss protecting unsecured-physical contact, in that if the Adversary were at the meeting, they would obtain meaning information about the clandestine operation. This chapter will focus on the virtual aspect of communications, both secure and unsecure. An example of a secure-physical contact, for those who are wondering, would be the use of a language unknown and inaccessible to the Adversary, including brevity codes.

The wonderful thing about technology, and smart people for that matter, is they turn things that are inaccessible to many into ubiquity. They automate manual and complex tasks, so other people do not have to perform them. While encryption used to take much time and effort and was only mildly secure, computers can now do much of this mathematical heavy lifting and the average person benefits from the results.

Regarding secure-virtual communications, protection comes from the use of encryption and steganography. Encryption makes the message unreadable, even if discovered, while steganography hides the message. With advanced technologies, anyone can set up technical surveillance and use tools to look for both encrypted messages and hidden messages. Encryption and steganography work in concert to ensure messages are secure.

Encryption without steganography may result in seeing the transmission of encrypted data. Encrypted data has a very distinct pattern, and therefore machines can easily flag the communication for review. While the security may be enough to keep the Adversary from gathering anything meaningful from it, the Adversary may choose to interrogate suspects for intelligence information, and in some circumstance, in very enhanced ways. The Adversary may not have the technical ability to break the Principal's communication, but they may have enough sadism to break the Principal's body, mind, or spirit.

Similarly, steganography without encryption is almost worthless if the Adversary is watching for its specific pattern. A technical Adversary can easily do this and the target will not know someone is watching him. Computers can read hidden messages in images as they pass through a network, or over the air, just like people can read the first letters of each line of a paragraph vertically. In this case, the Adversary would neither need to talk to their target nor would the target ever know someone compromised his communications, until someone hauled him off in the middle of the night.

This next section will go into the basics of encryption and steganography to best decide when and how to use it properly.

Encryption may eventually be completely worthless soon with the development of quantum and phase-shifting analog computers. Much of the encryption performed today relies on the mathematical manipulation of ridiculously large prime numbers, and how classical computing system cannot factor the resulting large semi-primes. This is not true with quantum or analog computers. These new computers can execute these algorithms, which computer scientists and mathematicians have developed, and decrypt these otherwise virtually uncrackable encryption methods. However, classic encryption is still a valuable tool, because:

Quantum and analog computing are still very new or expensive. As of this writing, the public is aware of only two quantum computers in existence, one of which some experts do not consider as a "real" quantum computer, and the phase-shifting memory analog computers are still theoretical. For these machines to decrypt communications, the sender or recipient would need to be the target of a very powerful government and very high on its priority list. For now, these machines will only decrypt other foreign government communications.

There are other methods to ensure that messages stay secure. One of the oldest and mathematically proven to be impossible to crack is the one-time pad. The problem with the one-time pad is that it is only as secure as the method of delivering the key. Once the Adversary obtains the key, then it can compromise the related message. If parties deliver the key over the internet, which uses SSL encryption, then the overall security is as secure as SSL.

The reason one-time pads are not ubiquitous in telecommunications is because of the key distribution issue. For clandestine operations, parties physically deliver one-time pads occasionally in either a drop or face-to-face meeting. If the Principal needs one-time pad level of encryption, then he should reconsider the operation. If the Principal finds it to be useful, then he should study them, which is not complex at all. One-time pad encryption is quite an elegant and simple security solution. Regardless, this is outside the scope of this book, as this information is readily available through a plethora of other sources.

Moving from the theoretical to the practical, most encryption methods, like those found in PGP, are enough to protect communications while conducting operations and for quite some time after. Therefore, the rest of this section discusses the more readily available technologies.

First, a quick lesson in encryption. Encryption involves three parts: the plain text, the algorithm, and at least one key.

The plain text is the readable message the sender wishes to send and therefore protects. If the Adversary gets a hold of this, then it may compromise the operation.

The algorithm is the logical or mathematical process in which the system turns something human readable and valuable into something useless. It takes the inputs of the plain text and a key, and turns it into what is known as the cyphertext. Then the decryption system takes the inputs of the cyphertext and key, and returns the plain text.

As the name suggests, the keys are what locks and unlocks the messages. Without keys, the cyphertext does not change or is impossible to decrypt. Being that classical computer systems are binary, everything is a series of bits, or "0s" and "1s". At the basic level, everything has a numeric representation whether it is text, photographs, videos, and so on. This means an encryption key can be anything digital and persistent. There are two primary manifestations of keys: single key and public-private key pairs.

Single keys both encrypt and decrypt messages. They can be a string of alphanumeric text or a token. Example of a string would be a password or passphrase and a token would be a file of random characters, a photograph, biometric data, or similar. Each have their own strengths and weaknesses.

Passwords and passphrases are the weakest forms of protection for two primary reasons: users usually restrict them to human readable characters and users tend to associate them personally. A higher bit-count for characters strengthens the key, because it forces the Adversary to try that many more different combinations. Characters of 256 different options need more time to try each one than characters of 100 options (keyboard).

Humans are not good at remembering meaningless and randomized letters and numbers. A user often thinks up a password that has some element of meaning. Even if it is a random word selected out of a dictionary, the fact it is a language the user knows is a vulnerability. The longer the password, the more likely the user associates it with something personal, like a favorite quote. This is the weakness. An adversary can use custom dictionaries catered to their target personally to crack even the most secure passphrases; however, that would need a bit of HUMINT.

Common cracking is trying various combinations of characters to guess the key. Without any intelligence, cracking can start with 0 and just increment into the vigintillions, remember: everything has a numeric representation. However, incrementing like that can take millennia, even with the world's most powerful supercomputers or botnets. It would be wiser to use some forethought and try the more likely combinations first. For passwords, it may restrict first tries to words in human languages. That may still take quite some time, so the Adversary may restrict the first tries to words, phrases, and combinations and character changes thereof, of favorite publications, events, persons, and so on in an attempt crack the password. Cracking passwords is more associated with cracking a person, instead of the method of encryption. If those attempts fail, the cracking attempt expands dictionaries for less personally known combinations.

However, proper passphrases are still quite secure. So much so, that many security services try other methods of cracking the encryption instead of trying these various combinations. Consider this: The average person knows about 35,000 words, and the average character count is 5.1 characters per word. With a phrase of 40 characters, there are about seven to eight words in this passphrase. If using a dictionary attack, and the Adversary did not know anything about the target, then it would still need 2.25 X 10 ^ 36 different combinations.

With a quad-core 4 GHz processor, all dedicated to cracking, it would still take 17 quadrillion millennia to try every combination. In terms of the most sophisticated super computer, it would take 767,811,830 millennia running through a basic dictionary and the various combinations thereof, and this does not include mixing languages, changing the character case, nor substituting numbers for characters or words. The trade-off is the fact that it must be 40 characters or more.

The best use of passphrases is to physically safeguard a computer system, offering a dual method of security. Encrypting the storage would safeguard the other keys used for communication over open mediums. While at this point, it would be true that this method would be only as strong as the passphrase. However, keeping the system hidden or safeguarded where others could not get to it can be more secure than the other hardened methods described below. The Adversary can only crack something on which they can get their hands.

Tokens are significantly more secure as they are files that have much greater lengths and use more of the character base-set. Take for example a bitmap file (photograph) that is 32-bit based, and is 12 Megapixels (4,000 by 3,000). Each pixel is one 32-bit based character, which means each pixel has 16.77 million options, and there are 12 million individual pixels. It would be pointless to try to brute force attack this, even with all the computing power in the world. It would be easier to just find the token.

The token is the vulnerability. It is often something tangible, whether it is a file on the system, in a card, or on a flash drive. Whoever bears this token has access to the protected system. Therefore, the Principal physically safeguards this token too. This usually means in a cache. If the Principal caches the computer system and the access token, then he uses two separate caches; otherwise, it is like hanging a key next to its lock.

Security conscious people widely uses the public-private key pairs, from the amateur to the professional, and for good reason: it is very secure. It allows the user to hand out a public key to send messages without worrying about the security of that key. If the Adversary gets a hold of the public key, then no harm done. The only key needing security is the private key, which the Principal limits physical access by safeguarding it in a cache.

All the characteristics of keys described above, with high bit character bases, and long strings still apply to these key pairs. This makes it quite difficult to crack, so much so, that the Adversary is likely to conduct another operation to get the information they need instead of trying to crack keys or encryption. They may just do some form of surveillance or interrogation to get the information they want.

Steganography is how to change the appearance of the encrypted message into something less obvious. Most cyphertexts will look obvious, as they are just random strings of text with headers and footers, and some formatting ques to make it machine readable. However, there are methods to conceal the message in other media. The three most common media containers are photographs, videos, and audio files.

Everything in a computer system has a numeric representation, and because it is a binary based system, these representations are integers. Even decimals are integers. Photographs, videos, and audio recordings are digital interpretations of analog sources. The difference in color of a photograph, while very minute, is still some definitive integer. This very small increment, whether it is the color of a photograph, or pitch and volume of an audio recording, the Principal can use it to write the bit of the message. This is known as the least significant bit. Changes to the last bit have negligible effects on the appearance of the original, so much so, many steganographic programs offer the least two significant bits to increase payload capacity.

There is a limit, and for a 12-million-pixel photograph, from a 12 MP camera, the message cannot be any longer than 46,875 characters, using 256-bit encryption, because it will turn every character in the message into a 256-bit character, and therefore each character in the cyphertext will use 256 pixels. If hiding a file, it can only be 45 KB. The smaller the image containers, then the smaller the cyphertext.

As mentioned before cyphertext often have headers, footers, and formatting ques, so the machines can recognize the file for decryption:

```
-----BEGIN PGP MESSAGE-----
Version: GnuPG v2


hQEMA5FHyv2O1fx1AQgA4tCFnBAhRV7p9bdoLn4QJLulZdD4Kv5fDXpWbOMwXats
cp5fX/MCRE/iZK2owTQoS6CfZHpRA2Hk4bkXqYNXq9t05pQEkaIbYzhYdQMVzE3f
RkYowz3cm1HGaRc3hPg437jQjLJ+v0/yxQgdgB/rP9og+3hdjnSKyY9WMK4kqhMO
bYqGzyHNxkSlK2IfKBHzEKL0PR8nwu/nojGl2pCzQ7m5XiWRzL8qM+Z94NapkL53
GaEDBgAmbhwuyYDUOW9W5hH+MfyUGPUf/U13lLiVBFGys1dXXz0t2CaPkCDPeggl
eoWatN5Upn1OxqyqCbAaji1ZYbf2Qm6UZKJ4bkd5l9LAZQGN7bMeBs9Xse+SHAFZ
K4/O+Y27WFwFwgSDcisnqnuUu1JUsNUFl1fEWUN9nYlNHrk+XLduZsy3OwuFx52B
BCINzjGPHoUCgB2sn/C3SO8sUwETzRhPAuGPaIH7D9PIRf4VE/OQ1iJUpJ0+77TK
69Qyx2ywRUJ+LhMMf8LjA3AJWj8wEiRp+QJmYNMxYma4qLoPKWWvCUbBhvCfTTWh
hgO9nkoL48uDipPl2a4JtKWwHqElAIrlvO2eOphA2612DQVU/OVjuF2Dsit5C/4h
S9XkF5iECjrqW4z7EujR6253YY2flUFe9e9en3DgkQhSm+2qNn+vbOHz20ZKvnEx
UnTxSU4jmzMnUvOS0huw6COwCyXJarVFcGAp2aNcmSpaQaubOQxY
```

=Rkd6

-----END PGP MESSAGE-----

Specially configured software can easily recognize this pattern. It has an obvious header and footer marking the beginning and end of the message, each line is 45 characters long, after which there is a line break, and finally the cyphertext block ends with "=Rkd6". If the Principal embedded this message in a media container, and passed it over an unsecured network, the Adversary may flag this message for further investigation.

To add another level of security, the Principal may strip these headers, footers, and formatting from the cyphertext before embedding it into the container image.

hQEMA5FHyv2O1fx1AQgA4tCFnBAhRV7p9bdoLn4QJLulZdD4Kv5fD
XpWbOMwXatscp5fX/MCRE/iZK2owTQoS6CfZHpRA2Hk4bkXqYNXq9
t05pQEkaIbYzhYdQMVzE3fRkYowz3cm1HGaRc3hPg437jQjLJ+v0/
yxQgdgB/rP9og+3hdjnSKyY9WMK4kqhMObYqGzyHNxkS1K2IfKBHz
EKL0PR8nwu/nojGl2pCzQ7m5XiWRzL8qM+Z94NapkL53GaEDBgAmb
hwuyYDUOW9W5hH+MfyUGPUf/U13lLiVBFGys1dXXz0t2CaPkCDPeg
gleoWatN5Upn1OxqyqCbAaji1ZYbf2Qm6UZKJ4bkd5l9LAZQGN7bM
eBs9Xse+SHAFZK4/O+Y27WFwFwgSDcisnqnuUu1JUsNUFl1fEWUN9
nYlNHrk+XLduZsy3OwuFx52BBCINzjGPHoUCgB2sn/C3SO8sUwETz
RhPAuGPaIH7D9PIRf4VE/OQ1iJUpJ0+77TK69Qyx2ywRUJ+LhMMf8
LjA3AJWj8wEiRp+QJmYNMxYma4qLoPKWWvCUbBhvCfTTWhhgO9nko
L48uDipPl2a4JtKWwHqElAIrlvO2eOphA2612DQVU/OVjuF2Dsit5
C/4hS9XkF5iECjrqW4z7EujR6253YY2flUFe9e9en3DgkQhSm+2qN
n+vbOHz20ZKvnExUnTxSU4jmzMnUvOS0huw6COwCyXJarVFcGAp2a
NcmSpaQaubOQxY=Rkd6

Now it just seems like a random string, and it may or may not be the natural state of legitimate media. However, the recipient must add these headers, footers, and formatting once he pulls the cyphertext from the image, so decryption software can recognize and decrypt it.

There is an important warning with the above examples: These are all human readable characters. Cyphertexts with 256-bit encryption have more options than there are human symbols, that is why opening a truly 256-bit encrypted file in a text editor will yield several blank boxes in the string. That is because there is no symbol representation for that numeric value. If the Principal uses encryption that results in some fully encoded cyphertext, then software can find it, because truly randomized digits, will result in some numeric values without an assigned symbol. This would need changing the string to return to its truly randomized state. Discussing this is outside the scope of this book.

Now, very smart people who find this interesting are continuously developing ways to defeat these programs that can identify and flag these containers, and as one team develops their technology, so will other teams. It is an arms race. Where the arms race is at any given point is difficult to pin down. The best practice is to live by principles. If the Adversary is technologically savvy, is actively looking for people like the Principal, and is watching for this type of communication, then the Principal does not use technical communications over publicly accessible mediums; he uses physical means of making contact, as described in the other chapters.

What this form of communication works well with is against scrutiny, it is a type of concealment device. If the Adversary searches the Principal, brings up the media, and opens files, then all they see is the digital container. To find whether there is anything suspicious embedded in the media would need a laboratory and data analysts. At this point it is about resource allocation.

The Adversary is neither going to deploy data scientists to investigate all arbitrary stops and searches, nor train those who do searches to be data scientists and field them with expensive equipment. The Adversary is going to rely on other indicators that will flag people as suspicious, and then go through his stuff. If the Principal can pass this first line of scrutiny, then he does not worry about cryptanalysis. Conversely, if the Adversary is performing cryptanalysis on the Principal's media, he has much bigger issues to worry about.

With this basic understanding of encryption and steganography, the next step is to find suitable tools that can perform these tasks.

One operating system to consider is The Amnesiac Incognito Live System or TAILS. The Principal can install it on a removable storage device, a USB drive, and can plug it into almost any consumer computer to run. After use, there will be no evidence of clandestine activities on that computer unless there is some malicious firmware operating in the background. The Principal does not need TAILS, as any operating system that can boot from these storage devices will work, but they would have to be custom built, which is outside the scope of this book. TAILS is an active project that is turn-key for what the Principal may need.

TAILS runs on removable storage and the system's Random-Access Memory. Once the power is off, all information on the memory is gone, leaving no evidence on the computer of clandestine activities. Only the removable storage device holds the compromising data. This is the only thing needing protection and the Principal can easily cache it.

While many use TAILS to securely communicate or compute on another machine, the Principal should use it with his own personal computer. This supports natural patterns of usage and avoids exposure to risks of using another person's computer. The machine stores no evidence, so if the Adversary gets a hold of it, they will not get any compromising files or programs. It is a way of keeping the cover life sanitized.

A choice in TAILS is persistent storage. This allows the Principal to keep files on the removable storage device, such as encryption keys and software. It sets aside some space on the device and encrypts it, so others cannot plug it in and see what is on it. The Principal uses persistent storage to keep the keys and steganography software readily accessible when needed. Persistent storage uses a passphrase to generate the encryption, so the Principal adheres to the principles relating to passphrases.

TAILS comes with OpenPGP, which many trust, and to their knowledge no intelligence agency has yet compromised it. However, no intelligence agency will publicize their ability to crack a system people trust. Regardless, if sophisticated and well-funded intelligence agencies concerns the Principal, then he should reconsider his goals.

TAILS does not come with steganographic software, which means the Principal must add it. If he uses TAILS, then the steganography software must be a standalone executable program. It should not need installation, only a file to run. Regardless of how the Principal installs and runs it, he must test the tools and equipment before he fields them. A quick Google search will yield a suitable list of available software. If the Principal does not trust publicly available software, then he must develop his own.

Due to the difficulty of finding whether the Adversary compromised the system, the Principal uses an air gap when dealing with compromising plain text. An air gap is when the computer system does not connect to a network. If there is malicious software on the machine, especially at the Basic Input Output System (BIOS) level, then it can start copying and sending data from what the Principal is doing to an adversary's server over the network. Ensuring the air gap keeps any communications that may hold the information from transmitting to adversarial servers. However, if the Adversary has infected the BIOS and is actively collecting from it, then the Principal has bigger issues, because the Adversary is now targeting him. This is just an extra step for security.

The process of ensuring an air gap is:

a) Boot the system into TAILS.

b) Disable the Wi-Fi modem, so the computer system does not connect to any networks, and ensure no wired Ethernet connections.

c) Upload or type the message, encrypt it, and sanitize the cyphertext (remove formatting).

d) Upload whatever media to use as a steganography container from its original storage device (camera memory card, USB stick), and embed the cyphertext. Overwrite the original source file with the new steganographic file, so there are no discrepancies.

e) Clean up the system by erasing the old documents, and ensure that no files transfer outside the computer.

d) Reboot the system without TAILS, and deliver the prepared communication however is most proper for the operation.

Now that the Principal securely packaged the message, the next step is to decide how he will deliver the message to the recipient. This is the difference between augmented and network based contact.

Augmented contact is one that does not use ubiquitous communication mediums. Whether it is a micro-dot, floppy disk, USB drive, MicroSD Card, or a specially calibrated photograph (think steganography), the medium is a physical device, which the Principal or Resident passes in a face-to-face meeting as described in another chapter. By far, this is the most secure in terms of technical surveillance, because the Adversary cannot surreptitiously copy it as it travels across the air waves or across a wired network. However, because it relies on physically passing the medium, it is susceptible to physical surveillance. Whether the Principal uses this will depend on the capabilities of the Adversary.

When it comes to network communications, neither the Principal nor Resident need to change the way they access the internet. The Principal does everything as normal. If the Principal or Resident post photographs to Facebook, Imgur, or any other social media site, then they should continue to do so. The difference is the occasional photograph of a beautiful landscape the Resident enjoys posting has a concealed message in it. They do not change any natural patterns when communicating publicly.

The Adversary could hire hackers, and while skills and access to systems may vary between hackers, basic hackers can still uncover quite a bit about a target's activities through technical surveillance of either the Principal or Resident. One such example, is if the hacker decides to infiltrate the home or work networks. They can see which sites the target visits and what he posts. If a target changes his patterns, then even a low skilled hacker may still spot these changes, which may lead to more scrutiny or hiring a better hacker.

While there are methods of countering this type of personal surveillance, like using Tor and going to open WiFi networks, the Principal should only do this after performing physical surveillance detection. The Principal avoids leading a technologically savvy and well-equipped Adversary to any location where he will behave differently than his natural patterns.

This is a proper time to discuss Tor. When most people think of the dark net and anonymity, some of the first thoughts revolve around Tor. To be clear, this is not a requirement for effective and secure technical communications, and depending on the circumstances, its use may pose a risk to operations, depending on how heavily monitored traffic is. If an internet service provider is actively watching the IP addresses and ports used by Tor, then it can very well compromise the operation.

Even if the Adversary is not working closely with internet service providers, they can set up several malicious Tor relays, and do cryptanalysis on those communications. Many people place a false sense of security into Tor, and thus accept a higher level of risk.

However, Tor does offer benefits. Primarily, free, and anonymous hosting. If the Principal must issue information to the public, then Tor may be the right choice while mitigating any retributions from the public message. However, that is outside the scope of this book. At this point of the clandestine operation, the Principal has a relationship with the Resident and they are not dealing with messages to the public.

If the Adversary has the capabilities to watch and analyze cyber communications, and they take it very seriously, then it is best to use another form of contact. The Principal may augment physical communications with encryption and steganography, but the Principal keeps the communications from the air waves or networks.

Lastly, making unsecured-virtual contact has a very narrow set of use cases in terms of security. The nature of communicating in such a way the Adversary sees or hears means that the Principal cannot mean what he says. This the nature of brevity. This is like a simpler version of creating a unique language or encryption, and thus the Principal teaches the Resident before its use.

The Principal should only use unsecured-virtual contact to start another, secure form of communication. The primary example of this would be to reschedule a contact, whether it was changing the location, day, or time of a physical meeting, or to notify the other party of an uploaded steganographic container. The Principal should plan these communications and schedule them at the last meeting to limit the frequency of contact. However, circumstances arise that need flexibility and the Principal will have some type of public facing communication to handle that.

Communications can either be persistent or scheduled.

Persistent forms of communication include those where the recipient constantly watches for communications, like a phone, radio, SMS, or application that notifies the recipient as soon as a message arrives. The recipient carries these devices always. Persistent is better, but not always possible.

Scheduled communications are those where the device is not on the recipient always, and the parties keep a schedule to ensure that the recipient checks the device at a specified time and duration. It is always a clever idea to have a backup scheduled form of communication. The means of communication should be already available to the Resident, so the Principal does not introduce foreign equipment into the Resident's life. If the Principal must give the Resident equipment, then a catalyst and cover must go with it.

When creating the brevity code, the Principal considers:

Covers: The discussions over unsecured communication mediums must fall within the context of the relationship. Codes like: "The eagle has flown the nest", have no place in the clandestine world, unless both parties are avid bird watchers, they are watching a specific eagle, it is very probable in terms of seasons and time of day that one of the parties just watched this eagle leave its nest, and that eagle and that nest is key to their relationship. Otherwise, the Principal is significantly more realistic about the topics of conversation.

Natural Dialog: The Principal only uses dialog that is natural. The Principal does not try to incorporate so much flexibility for variables he may or may not use. The Principal may name options to prevent unnatural dialog, such as Red for Tuesday at 12pm, Yellow for Thursday at 5pm, and so on. Attempts to incorporate specific date-time variables into the code, like referencing the book's series number and chapter as indicators of days and hours may not seem natural. This is unnecessary as many people have consistent schedules and the Principal does not take the Resident out of his natural patterns. There should not be a need to fine tune the specific times when the Principal knows the Resident's availability is the first Wednesday of every month after work between 5:00pm and 7:00pm.

If needed, the Principal names the options that coincide with the Resident's natural patterns, and shift that as many cycles as needed. This is also true for setting up various locations to meet. Sometimes the meeting venue becomes unsuitable. This can be due to higher popularity, development of a location since the Principal scheduled the meeting, or a shared internet site goes down. Having this backup ensure that the Principal will not have to approach the Resident again in an unsecured manner.

The conversation or message must make sense to anyone who is listening to or reading it. Reciting a bunch of arbitrary or random numbers is obviously clandestine activity, just do a search for "number stations". However, that is not what the Principal does and this section is discussing communications inside adversarial controlled area. If the Principal sets up a number station or similar, he would become a target very quickly. Instead, the Principal uses familiar words that were redefined to have operational meaning.

The Principal sets up some form of brevity to alter scheduled contacts in the event something comes up where the Principal must reach the Resident or vice versa, like an emergency. The Principal sets up at least one of each type of system: one technical and one non-technical. Technical includes public forums, underground radio transmissions, and so on. Non-technical includes something like an advertisement in a newspaper or a bulletin board. Regardless, both are easy to set up and offer an element of reliable redundancy to make or reestablish contact.

The key points to take away from this chapter are: understanding when using technical communications is proper (as concealment containers or if the parties are geographically separate), strong covers and normal behavior is of higher importance than using innovative technologies, and while these methods conceal information, it is still vulnerable to the physical world.

Drops are means for one party to pass information, materials, or equipment to another without making direct contact. The top reasons for using a drop are either exchanges in less permissive environments or exchanges between Residents. While there may be many reasons for using drops, the point is to use it when direct contact is not secure, possible, or proper.

In some of the most permissive environments drops may not be necessary, as face-to-face contacts could be secure enough to pass compromising materials; however, this may not be so in less permissive environments. In regions of the world where the indigenous are hostile towards clandestine relationships or operations, there exists a possibility that the Adversary or an agent thereof could interrupt the contact. When such a risk exists, it is best to keep compromising evidence away from direct encounters.

Sometimes one Resident needs what another Resident has. In such cases, especially when it is sensitive in nature, the less hands that touch it, including the Principal's hands, the more secure it is. It is still the Principal's responsibility to coordinate exchanges. The Principal should be the one who notifies the separate parties of when to load and unload the drops. If such coordination cannot take place, then it would be up to the Principal to take what would be one less-than-secure drop and turn it into two, more secure drops.

The Principal uses drops to pass contents that enable Residents to perform their specific tasks. When a Resident uses a drop, it is often to return the result of his assigned task.

Neither participants nor the drop can be under surveillance when unloading. Taking possession of compromising material under surveillance is unacceptable. Doing so may compromise the operation. However, loading a drop may be proper under surveillance, if surveillance cannot recognize the act of loading. Depending on what the Principal or Resident passes, security may be better if the contents stay in possession.

There are a few separate ways of executing the drop and the Principal uses each for different purposes. The circumstances of execution stay the same, but the method of loading and unloading may differ:

Dead drops are some of the most common types of drops. The Principal loads contents into a container and deposits it in a specific location. Some of the more defining characteristics of emplacing a dead drop is its precision. There is an exact location where the Principal or Resident places the container. Whether it is inside a toilet tank of an unfrequented restaurant or dangling from an external radiator of an archaic hotel, the placement of the drop is a matter of inches.

Mobile drops are a dead drop on a moving platform. This uses vehicles or persons on a predictable route. One party would conceal the contents with this unwitting person, usually their vehicle, as they traveled some known route. The other party, knowing where the unwitting asset will be, intercepts the contents. This is something that drug smugglers in Europe use to get contraband cross borders. They would conceal the drugs in the bumper or underside of a caravan, and after crossing the border, an associate would retrieve the contents. If authorities catch the unwitting agent, neither party cared: plausible deniability. The Principal can change this with the use of publicly accessible transportation, like ferries, buses, taxis, and so on. The moving nature of the package and how many people would come across it lends this method security. This is more difficult for surveillance, and much easier for the participants.

Tosses capitalizes on speed and fluidity of loading at the expense of precision. Where a dead drop may have a minute or two of seclusion, a toss is one second or a fraction thereof. If there is surveillance, then they are significantly less likely to see the drop. The down side is the other party must spend more time in the drop area looking for where the contents landed. These are the only way for higher risk or emergency drops where the possessor of sensitive contents must rid himself of them.

The following is the execution of a drop where the Resident transfers contents to the Principal. The planning of this should be such that the Principal knows when the Resident will acquire the contents for the drop. The Principal schedules this in an earlier meeting and the Resident executes the drop per the prearranged date, time, and location.

Just like any other means of communication, drops start with surveillance detection. Even if the Resident has some compromising materials, the only reason they had it, was because of their natural placement and access to said materials in the first place. There is still an element of plausible deniability when it comes to their possession, as a matter of mistake. Therefore, not all compromising materials will call for an emergency drop or destruction. If possible, the Resident returns the contents in an "innocent" attempt to rectify a wrong. Then the Principal decides whether to end the relationship with the Resident.

The counter-surveillance procedure is the same as others. The Resident enters an area where the Principal has command from an observation post and the Resident follows a route that will elicit surveillance behaviors. However, instead of making direct contact with the Resident after surveillance detection, the Principal sets up a signal site. This can be either some physical signal, where the Principal displays some discrete, albeit obvious signal to the Resident at a preestablished location, or uses a technical means.

If the Principal sees surveillance, then he does nothing. The Resident must only execute the drop if there is a "proceed" signal. If there is no signal, the Resident aborts and executes the instructions given to him. Instructions may include returning the contents from whence they came, destroying the contents in a secure manner, or executing an emergency drop. This will be at the Principal's discretion based upon the operational circumstances.

After the Principal signals the Resident, the Principal travels to the observation post of the drop. Upon seeing the signal, the Resident makes his way to one last cover stop in the area, before heading to the drop site. At the drop site, the Resident is to follow a specific route and be sensitive to other's behaviors. Despite checking for adversarial surveillance, the Principal's and Resident's next concern is the locals and their casual observation.

Obstruction must seclude the drop site from other causal passersby and obstruct the view from any potential observation posts. This means despite the observation post the Principal occupies having a general command of the area, it does not directly see the specific drop site. It should be in a spot where very few people, if any, frequent and if they do, the frequency is so rare the Principal and Resident should treat any other person's presence as a threat.

From the perspective of the Principal's observation post, the Principal can see the Resident's approach into the area and have enough time and distance to gauge other's reactions or responses to the Resident. Then in the final approach, the Resident ducks behind some form of obstruction from others in the area, loads the drop, and then exits from behind the obstruction and rejoins normal traffic.

The Resident then executes the load signal to show he loaded the drop. The signal site should be somewhere observable from the observation post. It does not necessarily have to be some persistent signal, like chalk on a mailbox, as behavioral signals, like lighting a cigarette, blowing one's nose, or walking away with hands in pockets, offer benefits of not leaving any evidence behind.

The Principal must encourage the Resident to abort the drop for any reason they feel the circumstances are unsafe. This can be the drop site is not as it should be or there were people present behind the obstruction. An example of the former is changes to the environment since casing. If the Resident is to deposit the contents behind a dumpster, but there are now two dumpsters, then the Resident should abort the drop, as it may cause the Principal to execute the unloading in an attention drawing way.

If the security concerns were temporary, then the Resident may try the drop again at a later prearranged time window, usually between 12 to 24 hours later, depending on the natural patterns of the Resident and what behaviors look normal. If not, or the next try fails too, then there should be an alternate or emergency drop site to get rid of the contents.

Once the Resident loads the contents into the drop and no security concerns exist, the Principal makes his approach to the drop site. He executes the unloading in a comparable manner to the loading and exfiltrates the area. If needs be, he uses the contents for whatever he needed them or caches it for later use.

Executing a drop in the opposite direction, from Principal to Resident, is very similar with just a few exceptions. Just as before, both parties should have set up a prearranged date, time, and location to start the counter-surveillance activities for the Resident before he tries to unload the drop.

As before any operational activity, the Principal executes counter-surveillance. Then the Principal gets the contents for the drop, usually from a cache, and loads the drop. The Principal must do this with enough time to get to the first observation post before the Resident arrives for surveillance-detection.

The counter-surveillance does not change. The Principal watches the Resident along the preplanned route and assesses the presence of surveillance. If there is, then he does not signal. If there is not, then he signals. After the signal, the Principal travels to the observation post at the drop site and watches the Resident approach, retrieve, leave, and display the unload signal.

If the Resident does not service the drop, then the Principal can try a similar time window for a second attempt. If that does not work or that is not possible, the Principal should retrieve it, cache it, and try again at another alternate location.

The Principal sets up an alternate means of communication in case the drop was not successful. This can be a brief encounter or technical contact where the parties quickly discuss and assess the mission. If the Principal loads the contents, but the Resident did not retrieve it, the Principal assesses whether it would be safe to check the contents at the drop. If the Resident feels there was surveillance, then the Principal returns only after assessing the area. If the Resident could not find the drop, but no threats exist, then the Principal may return to ensure it is still there. If it is missing, then it is time to reassess the operation, the relationship with the Resident, or both.

The following locations and routes need casing:

Observation posts are for the Principal to watch the Resident at cover stops during the counter-surveillance activities and the vicinity of the drop site. The Principal may have several observation posts because of visual limitations, or one well planned post. Drop missions can be in either rural or urban environments, so how many posts will depend on the specific locations the Principal decides are suitable.

The Principal must set up a legitimate cover for being in the area for the entire duration. This is particularly true of the observation post at the drop site. The Principal must watch the Resident and the others in the area to assess whether unloading can take place securely. The Principal must avoid the appearance of loitering, so he is not doing anything any longer than anyone else.

The loading and unloading approach routes for the Resident includes the path taken from the point from which the Resident will enter the intermediate area to the drop site. It includes a series of cover stops and legs that elicit surveillance behaviors. This is not as important for the Principal's approach, as he performed counter-surveillance before the drop.

The unloading route for the Principal is from the observation post to the drop site. The Principal executes this once the Principal sees the unload signal from the Resident and people are not paying attention to the drop site.

While there is nothing wrong with the parties approaching the drop from different directions, there is no need to do so. One could argue when people do similar behaviors, including approaching an unfrequented area from the same direction, it may raise suspicions. However, the Principal uses locations which obstruct observations. The location should have some obstruction from many angles, so as any loitering persons could not see multiple people doing something similar.

The safe signal site is mandatory if the Resident is the recipient of the drop and optional depending on the type of contents the Resident is loading into the drop. While the other methods of contact have initial contact points where the Principal meets the Resident, in the case of a drop, neither party makes face-to-face contact. Drops need a signal to let the Resident know it is safe to continue. The Resident must not see the Principal, so the safe signal to the Resident must be persistent enough for the Resident to see it until he passes by.

A drop site needs to be secure from other people. It should be readily accessible by anyone, so neither the Principal nor Resident are obvious when servicing it, but it should be of little importance to most people. The Principal ensures this with a location that is unfrequented by others and secluded from sight and sound of any potential passersby, but not so much it is illogical or surprising.

Demographics are important as the mere presence of the Principal or Resident can draw undue attention in the wrong areas. The more diverse the better, because people tend to abstract those of another demographic. If the demographics are identical, the prominent or identifying features of a person are likely noticed instead of their generalized, superficial features.

Public behavior is what most everyone else is doing. The nature of a drop is that there is a constant flow to its execution. There is very little, if any stopping to service the drop. The Principal avoids areas where people loiter for very long, if at all. Any loiterers should be gone by the time the Principal or Resident services the drop. People should be moving with some purpose, and often in transit from one place to another. They should be oblivious to the others around them. Even if the Principal uses unfrequented roads or paths, this criterion does not change. Even if there are few people present, those who travel through should not be interested in the area or behaviors around the drop.

Common behavior is not necessarily only what the majority does, but what a minority does too. Custodians or rummagers should not frequent the area. This is particularly important if the Principal uses certain alleys, public facilities, or public transportation. If these people are frequenting the area to clean up or rummage, then the Principal either reconsiders using it or uses a carefully cased schedule. If a party misses the drop, the Principal must then retrieve the contents before someone else does. Due to this added burden, the Principal avoids these areas.

Timing is naming how long the parties need to service the drop. This should be minimal for both emplacing and retrieving, but the Principal errors on the side of making it quicker and easier for the Resident. The purpose of timing is to minimize the potential observation of those who may see it. This mitigates risk.

Obstruction must be present with both loading and unloading. The Principal and Resident may use their body or vehicle as temporary obstruction, but the act must not be obvious. The Principal should find drop sites within some nook or cranny that will allow the Principal to temporarily move out of sight of normal traffic.

Logic addresses how odd or obvious the movement into the site would be. Ideally, a site offers an entrance and exit to allow the route through the site, but sometimes that may not be the case. If the site only has one way in and out, there must be an obvious, self-explanatory reason for using that location, preferably common knowledge. If not, then the site should have enough traffic flow that anyone who saw the Principal or Resident go in, should not be around to see him come out.

Contents play the largest role in deciding if a site is suitable. Much tradecraft development sought to miniaturize contents to fit in more places, so operatives can easily passed them securely, but sometimes that not possible. While true the advents of technologies have expanded the capacity of containers while shrinking their size, not every society has the material wealth to capitalize on such technologies. The Principal is still very much limited to the people with which he interacts. However, the more impoverished the society, the more rural it is. Significantly larger and more cumbersome contents are more easily hidden in the rural than the urban.

Emplacement and retrieval dictate the behaviors while servicing the drop. The smaller the container, the more options the Principal has and the more secure the drop. If the container is the size of a pack of gum, then it is much easier to conceal on the person. The Principal will have more places to conceal it at the location, making service much quicker, and thus limiting the risk of others seeing the drop.

The larger the container, the more difficult the service will be. Larger containers need better concealment containers when the Principal or Resident emplaces it, which means the Principal needs an even larger concealment device during transportation. If fabricating a softball-sized fiberglass rock, it would be obvious in a pocket or carried by hand. The Principal may need to carry it in a pack, which means loading and unloading will take longer and showing more extravagant movements. This means the site needs more seclusion.

If using a toss, then it may be easier to emplace the contents, but will be much more difficult and time consuming to retrieve the drop, unless the Resident tosses it into a vehicle like a brush pass of sorts. The best way of executing a toss is behind some natural screening around a bend in a secluded area, like a road in the rural or around a building in tight narrow streets. Retrieval will be difficult and will need to have enough time without anyone else in the area.

The Resident travels to the loaded or unloaded signal site next. It is often near the drop site itself, like just after clearing the obstruction of the drop site, where the Principal regains command of the Resident. Being that the Principal is watching the Resident, the signal needs neither to be persistent nor technical. A simple behavior or casually displaying an article will suffice. If the Principal is transferring contents to the Resident, then the Principal loads the drop before supporting the Resident's counter-surveillance.

The Principal may set up a load signal or combine load and safe signals at his discretion. The load signal notifies whether the Principal loaded the contents and whether the Resident should continue with surveillance-detection. No load signal means the Principal aborted the mission. However, the Principal may combine the safe signal with the load signal at the end of counter-surveillance. Using one signal alleviates operational complexity, but would need the Resident to execute surveillance detection before knowing whether the Principal aborted the operation. Conversely, having separate signals could save the Resident's surveillance detection route for another time.

Using the same drop repeatedly is not advisable. While professional intelligence agencies did this in the past, it has also lead to compromise. However, sometimes the routes are very strict and their options limited. This is the main reason the Principal tries to expand the natural patterns of the Resident: to support operational security.

Preparation is the next phase after selecting a proper site. There is a bit more to this type of contact than others, primarily due to the nature of handling compromising materials. Therefore, the following are some preparations to minimize some of the risks associated with drops.

The Principal gets the contents, which involves either coordinating an exchange between two Residents or by scheduling the retrieval from a cache, and transporting it to the drop. The focus of this is scheduling to minimize the time the Principal or Resident has these sensitive materials. However, the Principal never sacrifices making drops on time.

Acquisitions involve the Resident's natural access to the desired materials or information. This is also some of the most vulnerable activities, as making mistakes during acquisition triggers surveillance more than any other clandestine activity. This is the real genius work of the clandestine world. Unfortunately, the Principal cannot learn genius. The focus of any acquisition mission is understanding all the important obstacles and coming up with secure and innovative ways of overcoming them. Anything more into this topic is outside the scope of this book.

Prop acquisition is the sole responsibility of the Principal to ensure that those who need them, have them. In terms of drops, the Principal uses props to conceal materials in transit. These should fit the Resident's natural patterns and articles normally carried. If the parties will exchange a prop, then the Resident needs to carry an "empty" prop and exchange it for a loaded one. If the necessary props are not natural to the Resident, then his patterns need expanding with a suitable catalyst.

It is best the Resident obtains a prop organically, in that the he buys the article just as any other person. Special props, which the Principal must change to fulfill a special purpose, should come from common channels. The Principal and Resident should get identical props. One of which the Resident will have as a cover prop, and another the Principal will change into an operational prop. The Principal may set up a contact to exchange the cover prop for the operational prop if the Resident will load the operational prop.

Containers serve two purposes: to protect from the environment and to conceal from casual passersby. One container could satisfy both purposes or the Principal may decide to use two.

Depending on the contents, water and shock could very well damage the items inside if left outside for any duration or if conducting a toss. Therefore, the Principal should package contents in a way that will protect them. Regardless, the Principal must test the container thoroughly to ensure that the exchange will not destroy the contents inside.

Concealment does not necessarily have to be perfect, but the better it is, the safer. However, the level of craftsmanship must not be prohibitively high to be successful. There are two ways a concealment device hides in the environment: either independently, like rocks or trash, or dependently, like within, upon, besides, behind, or under a final reference point.

When designing independent containers, they must blend by appearing to be just like any common thing, but still offer some distinguishable characteristic that will allow the user to know it is the operational one. This does not have to be tricky. A fake fiberglass rock's weight will give it away. It can also be the containers position in relation to a reference point. Whatever the Principal decides, it must be unique enough to find easily and without error.

When designing a dependent container, the Principal does an exemplary job at casing the object which the container will match, if any part of it is visible from normal traffic. Human eyes are exceptional at finding inconsistencies in an otherwise consistent appearance. This can be a shiny finish among a dull backdrop, the slightest differences in shade or pigment, or a matter of fresh versus worn. However, the Principal can mitigate these risks by selecting a site that has poor lighting, sharp contrast, or much clutter. The recipient may find these containers by a detailed description of their location in or around the reference point.

The Principal considers the position the container will stay in waiting. In the rural, this is laying on the ground near a reference point and has some abnormality that will draw the observant recipient to it. However, placing drops on the ground is not always wise, as bending over to pick something up may draw attention, or take time. Historically, the use of magnetic boxes affixed to the bottom of a steel telephone booth shelf or hooks to hang a match box from a radiator were common. If the Principal places the container at a natural height where the recipient does not put himself in an unusual position, then it makes the service quicker and more secure.

Instructions for drops are more detailed than making direct contact. The Principal can divide direct contact instructions into digestible sets. For example, the first set is communicated in the earlier contact, which gives all the steps and behaviors for the Resident to get to the initial contact. Then at the initial contact, the next set is given to make the primary contact and it repeats again. With drops, the Principal passes all steps and behaviors to the Resident at once.

Specific instructions include the following:

The route will include both the method of travel and the reference points to guide the Resident to the drop. First is often naming an initial reference point, which is a commonly known point to orient the Resident to the area. Taking into consideration the Resident's normal means of travel, the Principal describes how the Resident will arrive to the area and where he will transition from a vehicle to foot. Then using a series of distances, directions, and reference points, the Principal describes the path the Resident will walk to the final reference point.

Pinpoint locations are specific locations out of normal view. These relate to the final reference point. If dependent on the final reference point, then the container is on, below, behind, around, or within this point. If the container is independent of the final reference point, then it is some distance and direction from the final reference point and another prominent point, like the ground, ceiling, walls, or other natural features. An example is: backside, near the rear-right corner of the refrigerator, approx. 4' above the ground.

The container description will either be its construction or for what to look. When describing a container for retrieval, the Principal only describes it enough to distinguish it from other objects. It can be as simple as "a green match-box on a hook". However, if something like a fabricated rock among real rocks, then the Principal describes the approximate size, color and the distinguishing feature built into it.

The Principal will derive the construction of the container from the casing, the desired characteristics (materials, size, shape, color, attachment method, distinguishing feature, and so on), how to source the materials and supplies, and how to test it. Again, if it is too complicated, the Principal builds it for the Resident, which has a way to insert contents into it, and he passes it to the Resident in a drop.

Time schedules are more about when the Principal expects the Resident to arrive in the area, and how long it should take him to get to the drop, service it, and leave the area. The Principal must know very well how quickly the Resident moves. The Principal does not schedule waypoints and actions which make the Resident appear uncomfortable, unnatural, or unusual to others. If the Resident is a slow walker, the Principal does not try to rush him, but plans the mission around this limitation. The point of keeping a schedule is to minimize exposure for the parties in an area.

Covers have two primary purposes: general and specific. General purpose is why the Resident is in the area. The Principal decides where, when, and why the Resident is going where he is.

Specific is the little deviation behind some obstruction or a momentary pause to service the drop. Examples include, tying his shoes, fixing his undergarments, lighting a cigarette, blowing his nose, using his phone, and so on.

Security considerations are either those activities that will draw attention, areas to avoid, or specific characteristics that would constitute warnings. Examples include: loitering in the presence of service staff, passing by a concierge desk, another paying attention to the Resident, or someone in direct observation of the drop.

Signals can either be technical or non-technical in nature, but will depend on the resources available to the Resident. The Principal puts non-technical signals in the Resident's path after a decision point and before exiting the area. Example are chalk marks, thumb tacks, or a piece of tape, which are now cliches. However, signals can be most anything that is easily modifiable or complimented, sturdy, and is only obvious to someone who is looking for it. This can be leaning a stick against a tree, a pattern of rocks, a tied ribbon, the presence of chewing gum, and so on.

Technical signals can be just as robust. Posting in a forum with specific verbiage, a specific image uploaded, an email, SMS message, or phone call. If the Adversary has robust technical capability, then the Principal alternates these signaling methods, to avoid showing a pattern before executing drops.

Rehearsals are important to ensure that loading or unloading happens as quickly and efficiently as possible. The Principal can only master drops by getting comfortable with the feel of devices, how to manipulate them properly, construction, and so on through practice. This often needs a replica of the key features in or around the proposed drop. If the container needs hung, then the Principal models the object and obstacles around which he will hang the container. If the Resident will construct the container, he must get those materials and supplies to practice and test. The Resident practices the steps of execution under the

Principal's supervision, so the Principal can spot and correct flaws before executing the drops in the field.

The key points to take away from this chapter are: understanding when using a drop is proper (less permissive environments), normal behavior, practice and fluidity is of higher importance than cover, and much planning and preparation is needed for communication than other means of contact.

www.ingramcontent.com/pod-product-compliance
Lightning Source LLC
Chambersburg PA
CBHW051448250726
48655CB00001B/311